HOW TO SELL YOUR OWN HOME

The Homeowner's Guide to Selling Property by Owner

WILLIAM F. SUPPLE, JR., Ph. D.

Picket Fence Publishing
Burlington, Vermont, USA

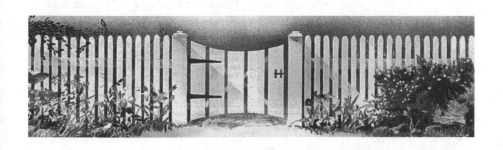

HOW TO SELL YOUR OWN HOME
The Homeowner's Guide to Selling Property by Owner

Published by:

Picket Fence Publishing Corporation
One Kennedy Drive
South Burlington, Vermont 05403
(802) 660-3167;   (802) 863-8965, fax
http://www.picketfencepreview.com

"This publication is designed to provide accurate and authoritative information in regard to the subject matter covered. It is sold with the understanding that the publisher is not engaged in rendering legal, accounting, or other professional services. If legal advice or other expert assistance is required, the services of a competent professional person should be sought." (From a Declaration of Principles jointly adopted by a Committee of the American Bar Association and a Committee of Publishers.)

Library of Congress Cataloging-in-Publication Data

Supple, William F., Jr., Ph. D. 1959-
   How to Sell Your Own Home:
   The Homeowner's Guide to Selling Property by Owner.
   Second Edition.
   160 pages, includes index.
   ISBN 0-9653911-1-6
   1. Selling your own real estate, home. 2. For-sale-by-owner real
   estate. 3. Personal finance.
Library of Congress Card Catalog Number: 96-70652
Printed in Canada

Contents

Chapter 4
Advertising and MarketingYour Own Home 51

Target marketing • Advertising methods • Determine a budget • Researching the advertising alternatives • Yard signs • Characteristics of an effective sign • What to expect from a sign in the yard • Print advertising • Classified ads • Photo classified ads • For-sale-by-owner real estate publications • Open houses • The internet • Where the buyers are • The right advertising mix

Chapter 5
Showing Your Home:
How to Interact with Buyers 67

How to deal with buyers over the telephone • Answering machine messages • Information to give & receive from buyers over the phone • Drop-ins • What to have available for the showing • Fact sheet • Financial worksheet • Seasonal photo album • The approach to take when showing your home • The successful buyer visit • The style to use when showing your home • What if they don't make an offer or call back? • The buyer's point of view • How to create demand for your home

Chapter 6
Negotiation:
Specific Terms and Conditions of the Sale 85

Avoiding confrontation • Basic elements of negotiation • Preparing to negotiate • What to expect during the negotiation process • Common items and terms subject to negotiation • Sales price • Response time limit • Deposit • Who holds the deposit money? • Financing • Possession & transfer of title • Who pays for which items at settlement? • Sale contingent on the buyer selling their current home • The property appraises for the purchase price or more • What personal property is included in the sale? • Sale contingent on the house passing inspections? • Consider what happens if the house "fails" the inspection • Rent back provision • Overview of the negotiation phase

Chapter 7
The Legal Aspects of Selling Your Own Home   97

Choosing a lawyer • What does a lawyer do in a real estate sale? •
Draft and review the sales contract • Conduct a title search (buyer's
attorney) • Help you meet the terms and conditions of the sales contract
The closing • Sequence of events at the closing • Timeline of events
from the signing of the contract until the closing • Purchase and sales
contract

Chapter 8
Home Inspections   105

Guidelines in choosing a home inspector • Mechanics of a home
inspection • The exterior • The interior • Property information report

Chapter 9
Mortgage Basics for Sellers   117

Conventional loans • Fixed rate • Adjustable rate mortgages • Government-backed loans • Federal housing authority loans • Veteran's
Administration mortgage loans • Direct seller involvement in financing
Buy-down the interest rate • Closing assistance • Lease-options to
purchase • Pre-qualifying your buyer • Mortgage loan pre-qualification
chart • Timetable of the mortgage process

Chapter 10
Dealing with Real Estate Agents   127

Types of real estate agency listing contracts • Exclusive right to sell •
Exclusive agency • Open listings • Flat fee arrangements • Discount
real estate services • Temporary listing contracts • Buyer brokers • Bad
buyer brokers • Good buyer brokers • Questions and answers about
real estate • Teacher gives real estate agents below-average grades on
ethics • Article on FSBOs was slap in face to real estate companies and
agents

Introduction

Home ownership is part and parcel of the American Dream. Owning your own home also means that sometimes it becomes necessary to sell that home and move on...hopefully into a more desirable, more valuable home. This book is designed to help you, the homeowner, effectively and professionally market and sell your own home now that the time to sell has arrived. Selling by owner, with no real estate agents involved, will save you the expense of sales commissions. Depending on the sales price and the amount of the commission in your area (anywhere from 6-10%), avoiding real estate agents can help you avoid spending thousands or tens of thousands of dollars needlessly. Plus once you learn how to sell your present home, you will have a skill that will save you thousands of dollars on every move you subsequently make in the future!

My wife and I are not real estate agents, or financial experts or mortgage brokers. We're homeowners, just like you. Actually, we had no relevant experience in anything even remotely related to real estate before we started in the for-sale-by-owner business. I was a neuroscientist, and my wife was an advertising and marketing executive. When it came to real estate we were just consumers: a couple trying to find a new home for our growing family. We were looking with real estate agents at homes for sale through the multi-list service. To make a long story short, we quickly became frustrated with the whole process. We would see an out-of-focus black and white rendering of the exterior of a home, go out to see it and be disappointed and angry because we were wasting our time. We just wanted more information about a home so we could decide if it was a possibility before we went to inspect it. Let's see more photographs of the home, let's have more of a description of the home's features, let's have a more attractive presentation of the property than just the blurry listing sheet. That's what we wanted! Unfortunately, that was not the way traditional real estate works.

So the more frustrated we got, the more we realized that there was an opportunity to change the home shopping process from our perspective (the buyer's) for the better. So we established our magazine, *Picket Fence Preview*, which advertises homes offered for sale by owner. The magazine was designed to appeal to buyers - giving them lots of information about the homes and showing multiple photograph spreads of the homes including interiors! We thought that a magazine designed to appeal to the buyer would in turn, appeal to the seller. Our beginnings in this business really could be summarized as a "necessity is the mother of invention" situation. We saw a need and filled it.

Soon after publishing the first issue of our magazine, we started getting lots of questions from our homesellers and their buyers. The questions ran the gamut from pricing to legal issues related to selling a home. Since we had no experience, we realized that we couldn't fulfill this need for expert real estate advice, so we organized educational seminars on how to sell your own home. The invited speakers were the experts: a real estate appraiser, a real estate lawyer, a mortgage loan officer, and a home inspector. They described their roles in the home selling and buying process and answered questions.

We began to acquire lots of experience: we learned from the seminars and from our experts. Most importantly we learned from our customers- the homeowners selling their own property in our magazine. They taught us what was effective and what wasn't. We listened and compiled the information we learned from these thousands of homesellers and organized it into this book. *It is our experience with the actual people selling their own homes that makes this book radically different from all others on the topic.* This experience, knowledge and testimony from thousands of other for-sale-by-owners, and our analysis and synthesis of those collective experiences is what we have to offer you. This book is a practical and functional guide to selling your own home. And it's written from the perspective that is most useful to you: *yours*.

The most consistent and pleasantly surprising fact we have learned is that selling a home is relatively simple, once you know what to expect and how to prepare. This book teaches you what to expect and how to prepare. Think about it! You have a desirable piece of property, a home, that lots of buyers want. You want to sell, they want to buy, what could be simpler: it's like the opposite poles of magnets, they naturally will connect.

So why don't more people sell, or even try to sell their own homes? Because they erroneously think it's too complex or they're intimidated by the process. It's ironic that people are intimidated by a process they know very little about. The objective of this book is to present the steps involved in selling your own home in a clear and concise manner. Knowing what's involved will help to educate you about what to expect, and how to prepare and will work to demystify the selling process. We trust that you will learn, as many a for-sale-by-owner has learned by experience, that the secret to selling your own home is that...there are no secrets at all. Once you know what to expect and how to prepare, an attractive, fairly-priced home will sell itself when properly advertised! You will benefit from the acquired experience of other for-sale-by-owners who have been in your shoes before.

How this book is organized

It is important to keep in mind that most of the information contained in this book was gathered from real-life experiences...the experiences of homeowners, just like you, who were selling their own homes. This practical, "from-the-field" information just isn't available in any other book. What also helps to make this book different is that at strategic points there are direct quotes from successful private homesellers giving advice to you. Think of this information as Homeowners Helping Homeowners, like neighbors exchanging information across the fence that separates their yards. We hope you'll find the tips useful and insightful, and we know you'll be inspired and motivated by them.

To help you along, we've included worksheets and forms that will help you get organized and keep you on track as you embark on the rewarding process of selling your own home.

The major addition for this Second Edition is Chapter 12, *Steps involved in buying a home.* We have received comments from home sellers that while they felt they knew what they were doing after reading this book, they weren't so sure that their buyers knew the first step to take. Chapter 12 presents in a simple step-by-step manner what a buyer should do if they want to buy your house. Often, the first step is the hardest one in any process. This chapter answers the questions: We want the house, now what do we do? You may want to make this chapter available to your buyer to help them along the road toward buying your property.

This book, though written by me, would not be possible without the thoughtful discussion and keen insights offered by my wife and business partner, Toni. I would also like to thank other for-sale-by-owner publishers and friends for their advice and comments that helped improve the material that's presented here in this Second Edition: Robert Tully, Wappingers Falls, NY; Charles & Susan Samsonow, White River Jct. VT; Bob Balander, Albany, NY; Sam Maxey, Roanoke, VA; Joe Wood, Memphis, TN; and Jim Vogelpohl, Portland, OR

Good luck and happy reading!

WF S

Chapter 1

Trends in For-Sale-by-Owner
Real Estate

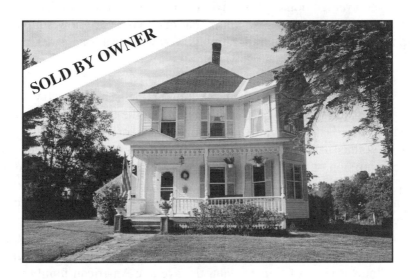

"Selling a home is not rocket science or brain surgery. It's a real do-able thing between reasonable people" -- Pat Burds

Thinking of selling your own home. You're not alone. More and more homeowners are choosing to sell their own property for many reasons both financial and practical. We don't have to tell you how much of your hard-earned equity you can save by selling on your own. In fact, many personal finance experts have argued that it's almost impossible not to save money selling by owner compared to selling your home through a real estate agent. What may be somewhat surprising to you is that selling on your own, compared with using a real estate agent, can be much more convenient, less stressful and much, much more likely to accomplish your ultimate goal of selling the property.

In the chapters ahead we will take you step-by-step through the entire process of selling a home. You will learn how to prepare for the selling process and what situations to expect when selling your own home. Our experiences as the publishers of a for-sale-by-owner real estate magazine have provided us with important insights into what you need to know to effectively sell your own home. Therefore, we have concentrated our efforts into a comprehensive, step-by-step description of the home selling process for the average homeowner. We assume no prior knowledge, special experience or background. We know that once you learn how simple and straightforward a real estate transaction is, you will always consider, as your first and best option, selling by owner.

Your home is probably the single most valuable asset you own, comprising the majority of your net worth. Now that the time has come to sell, selling it yourself can save you a substantial amount of money (literally thousands of dollars in real estate sales commissions). As an example, a 6% sales commission on a $200,000 property is $12,000, twelve thousand dollars! That money can enhance the comfort of our retirement or make the downpayment on a larger, more expensive home, or form the basis of a college fund.

The sooner you learn how to sell by owner the better. According to United States Bureau of Census data, the average American family moves once every five years or so. Even if your family moves only three times, the cumulative savings from selling by owner could add up to very large numbers. In fact, we've heard from many of our customers that they were able to afford "more" house on their next purchase because they sold their previous home on their own.

"In essence, we would not have been able to afford another home if we got our price (for this place) and had to pay a real estate commission on top of it"-- Pat Burds

"The fact that we didn't have to pay a realtor's commission allowed us to build our dream home, with every detail we wanted!"-- Ben Hale

As a general guideline the information presented here is divided into three segments that discuss and explain: 1) How to prepare your property and get yourself ready before you place your home on the market; 2) How to "sell" your own home; and 3) What to expect and do after you get a deposit and until the deal is closed. The information covers the logical time frame of the homeselling process from start-to-finish: what to do before you put your property "on the market", how to attract and interact with buyers during the selling period, and how to make sure the deal is completed or closed after you've received a purchase deposit on the property.

All of this information is necessary because it's up to you, the homeowner, to understand the process and keep the deal on track until the closing. It's important for you to understand that most buyers will have little or no experience in buying or selling homes, so it's up to you play the role of the expert and to help your buyer along. You must be able to ensure that your buyer understands the steps necessary for them to purchase your home! We believe that once you see how simple selling a home is, you can go forward with the confidence that you *can* easily sell it yourself and save your equity.

For-sale-by-owner real estate

The for-sale-by-owner movement that is sweeping the country is happening for several very simple reasons. First of all, buyers are smart, they know that without a middleman involved (a real estate agent) they will probably get a better deal directly from the homeowner. Buying direct is always less expensive. Witness the growth of Office Depot, PriceClub, WalMart and Sam's Club as a testament to the demand by consumers for direct access to the price advantages that wholesale offers.

Selling by owner is also an option open to homeowners who are frustrated with the lack of effectiveness of their real estate agent in success-fully selling their homes. Let's face it. If a homeowner inflated the price of their home to compensate for a real estate agent's commission they have placed themselves at a competitive disadvantage compared to a for-sale-by-owner homeseller. They just aren't price competitive (unless they listen to the agent and continue to drop the price). In many parts of the country prop-erty is not appreciating in value at the rate it once did, and in some markets real property has even declined in value. Just like you, more and more homeowners have come to realize that 6 -7% is just too much to pay to have someone market your home for you!

To illustrate this point, let's use the type of numbers that are associated with home sales. Say you have a home that's worth $150,000, if you have an agent list your property at 6% commission, you'll end up paying $9,000 as a selling fee. That's a lot of money! You can compensate by asking more for your property, say $155,000 or even $159,000 to cover the commission, but now you've lost your competitive edge. Your house may sit on the market, your agent will nag you to drop your price and meanwhile...your neighbors down the street will have already sold and moved up because they sold on their own and could afford to ask $150,000. Homeowners not having success with agents can be more price-competitive selling by owner and can still retain a larger share of their equity.

Another important factor contributing to more and more homeowners selling privately is the first-time homeseller. These homeowners bought their house at the peak of the market in the 1980s and have not benefitted from low interest rates or substantial price appreciation. They have to sell on their own because they can't afford to move if they also have to pay an agent's commission. That 6 or 7% commission is a major portion of their equity... in some cases, the sales commission can be 100% or more of the homeowner's equity. So in this unfortunate situation, the sellers actually would have to pay thousands of dollars out of their pocket to sell and move on!

And finally a major force driving the for-sale-by-owner real estate movement is that sellers are becoming more educated and smarter. They know that most HOMES SELL THEMSELVES and with the amount of money at stake, it's a smart money move to learn how to sell it yourself. Many homeowners remember the details of the transaction when they bought their home they are now about to sell. If you're like most people you feel that the agent's involved didn't do much to earn those thousands in commissions and will do things differently next time. Next time is here! A recent survey reported in the *Wall Street Journal* found that of the homesellers who *attempted* selling their own home, over 93% were successful. The range of savings reported by these homesellers was from $3,500 to $31,000! So you can be successful selling your own home. More and more people are doing it and you'll do it too.

The for-sale-by-owner real estate movement

We have referred to the for-sale-by-owner movement several times now, and perhaps we should explain what we mean by that. We were somewhat surprised by the number of buyers and sellers who told us how pleasant it was to deal directly with each other face-to-face. This was, of course, in comparison to their prior experiences in which real estate agents were involved. We've even had people report the development of new friendships with the people they met as potential or actual buyers of their homes. There is definitely the development of a "partnership mentality" between the seller and buyer, both striving for a mutual goal. Cooperation and working toward a common goal best describes the attitude we've encountered.

Through our discussions with other for-sale-by-owner publishers, we found similar situations to exist between the buyers and sellers in private transactions all across the country. So we view the for-sale-by-owner real estate movement as a grassroots movement: individual sellers and buyers striving for mutual beneficial goals. Without agents involved you can achieve these goals less expensively and far more efficiently.

The movement is also growing because of the availability of useful information about the selling process. People are learning that it's easy; you just have to make the commitment and you're very likely to succeed. The staggering number of private transactions has also been noticed by other industries associated with the purchase and sale of homes. For example, a recent article in *The New York Times* described the growing interest of the mortgage lending community in the for-sale-by-owner movement:

...one in three homes sells without the intervention of a broker. Those people who bought high in the '80s and are selling low in the '90s see the elimination of sales commission charges as one way to cover their outstanding mortgage debt on the property-or at least cut back on their losses. The idea is gaining credibility from the swelling ranks of financial planners like Duncan Demoss of Westlake Village, CA, who recommends the concept (selling by owner) as a smart money move. "There's a rebellion going on out there," said Mr. Demoss. Mortgage lenders stung by the end of the refinance boom and thus eager to increase business are also aggressively promoting the idea of people selling their own homes.
Andree Brooks, New York Times, Nov. 13, 1994

The concept of selling by owner makes good practical and financial sense to most homeowners and that's where the movement derives its strength. In the near future, as more people attempt and succeed in selling their own property it will quickly become the main method of sale.

Finally, the knowledge we have acquired about the for-sale-by-owner process (e.g. how easy it is, how many people are actually successful, buyers and sellers becoming friends, etc.) is in stark contrast to what the real estate brokerage industry falsley teaches: that it's difficult to sell real estate. As we stated in the Introduction, we had no prior experience in real estate before we started our magazine, we were just homeowners searching for a new home. Our "discoveries" about for-sale-by-owner real estate stand out prominently in our minds because they violated what we though we knew about real estate. In fact, when we examined where we got the information that helped form those beliefs, the "facts" were always from a common source - the real estate agents and brokers themselves! In fact, most of what the average person "knows" about real estate comes from real estate advertising. Most of this advertising is designed to make the selling and buying process appear as complex as possible thereby justifying the need for a real estate broker. In Chapter 10, we will show you some of the "tricks" that real estate agents use to discourage for-sale-by-owners by making the process appear complex and mystifying. Interestingly, these tactics are endorsed by the National Association of Realtors, a $24 billion lobbyist organization, whose mission is to promote the real estate industry and consequently discourage homeowners from selling by owner.

Eight advantages of selling your own home

The following describes some of the main financial and practical reasons for selling your own home. Some are quite obvious, some may be surprising. We feel it's important to learn these points because they will help you understand and critically evaluate the information presented in subsequent chapters. Also some buyers may be under the influence of the myths that real estate agents promote as to why they want to steer clear of for-sale-by-owners. For example, for-sale-by-owner's are difficult to deal with, or an agent will get them a better price (interesting, since agents usually work for sellers). Furthermore, knowing these arguments will help steel you against the doubts that real estate agents may try to foster in your mind as you're selling by owner.

1. To save large amounts of money

Why spend money when you can avoid it? Selling by owner is a good way to save your equity by avoiding expensive real estate sales commissions. A 6% commission on a home that sells for $150,000 is $9,000. Think of that $9,000 as a *selling cost*. It is helpful to consider the potential commission savings as a factor in a simple cost/benefit analysis when deciding to sell your own home. Do you think it will cost you $9,000. in out of pocket expenses to sell your own home? Most likely it will cost you a small fraction of that. And remember that when you sell your own home your selling costs (advertising, signs in the yard, etc.) may be tax-deductible, further reducing your out-of-pocket expenses (call the IRS 1-800-829-1040 and get Form 2119 Expense of Sale form for the current tax year).

In fact, you would be hard-pressed not to save money when selling by owner compared to selling through an agent!

2. To sell faster

Selling your home with an agent may actually *delay* its sale, contrary to what agents' advertising may say. Consider the common practice of inflating the price of the home to compensate for the agent's commission. (It's a practice because it's how agents are taught to price homes in their training manual *Modern Real Estate Practices*). In the first place, a buyer knowing you're using an agent won't pay the inflated price so they will reflexively offer less. Now you must choose between accepting less, losing more equity or waiting for a buyer to pay the inflated price...*all undesirable*. An overpriced home will sit on the market for a longer period of time. Eventually buyers will think there is something wrong with the house otherwise it would have sold by now and it may never sell.

In fact according to the real estate industry's own statistics, up to 60% of all homes listed with real estate agents do not sell within the listing period which is typically 6 months to a year. In these unfortunate cases, either the listing expires or the owner gets discouraged and takes it off the market.

> *Ben Hale, a private homeseller, found that in a head-to-head competition with a local real estate company, he reached the finish line before his agent ever left the gate: "I sold my house myself within 6 days (using your magazine)... for my asking price, and with two back-up offers as well. My realtor never brought a single person to see it, though he'd listed and advertised it in the paper with a photo, and at the same price, for a month before me!"*

3. Greater market immunity

What we mean by this is that selling by owner makes financial and practical sense in both buyer's and seller's markets. In buyer's markets, with lots of similar homes available, it can be difficult to sell because of the competition. Selling by owner gives a competitive advantage to that homeowner because they can afford to be more price-competitive, if they choose, than their neighbor listed with a real estate agent. All other factors being equal, common sense economics predicts that the buyer will prefer the comparable, though less costly home offered for-sale-by-owner.

In seller's markets, where the buyers' demand for homes outstrips the supply, it's not smart to pay a commission and sacrifice any portion of your equity. Knowing how to sell by owner will enable you to retain the maximum amount of your hard-earned equity. The good practical sense of selling by owner works in both types of markets.

4. Convenience

YOU are in control when you sell on your own. You schedule your own appointments for buyers to visit. No more having to keep your home spotless just in case an agent decides to show it that day. No more leaving the house because an agent wants to show it. No more personal security threats from lock boxes and unannounced visits from agents. When selling your own home, you know when people are coming for a visit, and can prepare accordingly. In fact, we were somewhat surprised to learn from our customers that the **convenience** of selling by owner was often a major factor in their decision to drop their real estate agent and sell their own property.

"One of the nicest things about selling on our own was that we were in control of the showing schedule. We didn't have to leave the house in the morning and wonder if people were going to look at it. We had an answering machine-people called- we called them back and would set up a time at our mutual convenience" -- Ben Hale

5. Less stress and frustration

Change is almost always stressful. The events surrounding the home selling and buying process involve major changes so anticipate stress. And you are getting stress from both sides because you are also probably looking for a new home at the same time as trying to sell your current property. Rest assured that since you are in control when selling your own home you will experience much less stress than you would if were selling through a real estate agent. Since you will know how much effort is being put into marketing your home, you won't get frustrated because "they're not doing enough." And since you meet prospective buyers you know how interested they are and won't be in the dark wondering what's going on. This direct feedback is easier to live with than is wondering how things are going, or worse, why no one has made an offer yet.
Control = less uncertainty = less frustration = less stress.

6. You can sell your home best

It's safe to say that no one knows a home better than the current owner. After all, you've probably lived there for a number of years. You know your home inside and out, the schools, the neighborhood, the tax base and what is special about the area and your neighbors. A well-maintained, fairly-priced home will virtually sell itself; your role is simply to embellish information and help present the property in its best light.

7. Exclusive and special homes

By definition, homes offered directly by owner are exclusive and special. They aren't listed with real estate agents or available anywhere else, except from the owner. This situation generates a heightened sense of urgency for the buyer to see your home first, before it is purchased by someone else. Buyers throughly search advertising publications for new properties listed for-sale-by-owner for this reason and, of course, for the better deals offered. In our experience, we have learned that the most desireable homes are offered for-sale-by-owner because the seller realizes that the home will *sell itself* if properly advertised.

8. Selling your own home is EASY.

The rest of this book will show you how easy it is to sell on your own. There are no "secrets" to selling a home. In a manner of speaking, the secret is that there is no secret! What we've learned from our experiences with thousands of for-sale-by-owner homesellers is that **HOMES SELL THEMSELVES**. Attractively present your home, price it fairly and consistent with your market, effectively advertise it, and you will be in a great position to sell your own home and save your hard-earned equity.

With such attractive financial and practical arguments for selling by owner, why doesn't everyone sell privately? One barrier, in addition to the real estate industry itself, to selling on your own is purely psychological: the fear of the unknown...of trying something new. Some people think that the process is too complicated when in fact most real estate transactions are quite simple. As you go through this book, you will learn about the process and see how simple it is, and consequently become very comfortable with selling by owner. Like most new things, people are initially reluctant to attempt something new or unknown, but once they learn about the homeselling process it is demystified and becomes an easy goal.

By considering each of the points that follow, you can become more informed and that will go a long way toward building your confidence so that you can sell your own home.

"If you've sold your own car, you can sell your own home...it's that simple!" -- Dominick St. Pierre - who sold his own home five times.

What it takes to sell by owner:
Make the commitment to sell on your own

Making commitments involves understanding what's involved and then developing realistic expectations about the process.

Time on the Market: The first step is developing realistic expectations about the real estate market in your area. Find out how long it takes to sell a home in your price range, in your area or neighborhood. Check with your neighbors, ask a real estate appraiser. For example if in your area the average length of time a home is on the market in your price range is 3 months, then 3 months is a realistic expectation for how long it might take to sell your home. It's critically important that you enter the for-sale-by-owner process with a reasonable expectation of how long it will take to sell a property like yours. The danger in not establishing a good estimate of how long it may take is that you could get prematurely discouraged because you expected it to sell fast, when in fact it will take 3 months. What we have learned is that sellers with unrealistic expectations become discouraged too soon, and are vulnerable to listing with a real estate agent. The irony is that when they list, usually at a higher price than for-sale-by-owner, the home has an even less likelihood of selling! So do yourself a favor learn how long to expect and plan on it taking that long. If you should sell faster than expected...great.

When considering how long it may take to sell be sure to factor in the time between when you find the buyer and when you move out. There are built-in, almost unavoidable time contraints (perhaps it takes 8 weeks to get a mortgage, 3 - 4 weeks to get an appraisal). The amount of time will vary with the region of the country you're in and the activity in your local real estate market. If your home is in a good location and priced right, you can probably sell it faster than the "average" amount of time; if not, it might take longer.

"When I put my house on the market I anticipated it would take between 5 - 6 months...so I had budgeted for that time-wise...but it only took a week!" -- Ben Hale

Budget for Selling Expenses: Expect to spend money to sell your home. Most businesses plan on spending a certain amount of money to advertise their goods and services to the public. The return on that investment will vary depending on lots of factors, but most businesses could not survive without some sort of effective advertising program. The for-sale-by-owner homeseller is no different. You will need to become somewhat sophisticated in understanding how advertising works and how to capitalize on the advantages available to you when selling your property by owner. It will cost you some money to sell your home. The fact is that spending a little up front will save you a lot at the closing. People selling their own homes must recognize that it costs money to advertise to bring in buyers, get legal representation with the contract and transfer the property. All of these costs combined will be a small fraction of a real estate agent's commission.

So the choice you have to make is simple: you can pay a little now (selling on your own) or pay a lot later (commission fees). We have found that successful private homesellers avoid the trap of "being penny-wise, and pound-foolish." While homesellers who are vulnerable to real estate agents are!

"The idea is not to nickel-and-dime it but to really plan on spending some money on the advertisement. If you're going to pay $15,000 to a realtor-there's a lot of advertising money there, that's the way we looked at it!" -- Jeannie and Dominique St. Pierre

The deal revolves around you

It's important for you to realize that the sale of your home revolves around you. You can consult a host of experts, books and videos to understand the mechanics of the transaction but ultimately *you* have to coordinate the process and make the deal happen. As you learn most of these tasks require nothing more than telephone calls. If you're too lazy to make a few phone calls you should stop here and call your friendly local real estate agent they'll be happy to take your money.

The following chapters will educate you about the process of selling so you know what to look for so that details don't go unattended. A little effort on your part will be greatly rewarded with the highly satisfying personal and financial experience of selling your own home.

What is your situation?

Specific segments of the information presented here will be more or less relevant to you depending on your specific selling situation. Consider the next important section on pricing, for example. If you are in no particular hurry to sell your home, you may be able to offer a somewhat higher price (within reason) and sit tight and wait for a buyer willing to pay top-dollar. If you are more motivated to sell, perhaps you are being transferred in a few months, then you probably need to be more price-competitive than your neighbor with time on his side. There will be many instances where the suggestions offered regarding selling should be tempered with the knowledge of your own unique situation. Generally, the more urgent it is for you to sell, the more willing and able you'll need to be open to negotiation (this includes price, conditions of the sale, incentives, etc.). But also keep in mind that no matter how urgent it is for you to sell, you can be more price-competitive than someone selling through a real estate broker and since you're in control, you know how much effort is being put into the marketing and promotion of your home.

"I didn't know what the outcome was going to be but I figured I had nothing but time...so I gave it a shot." -- Ben Hale

"We really weren't in a hurry, we didn't have a deadline that we had to be out by...We had more time than we had money, that was really the issue" --Pat Burds

"I love to fix up a home, decorate it and then find someone who will

appreciate it and then go on to another one."--Jeannie St. Pierre

"When we had our house listed with a real estate agent I think we had around 50 people come to see the house...but nobody was really interested. So we decided after 6 months it was really time to take things into our own hands and do it ourselves!" Graciella Callas

The tasks involved in selling a house can be easily accomplished by an organized, determined seller aided by key professionals who have a vested interest in facilitating your for-sale-by-owner real estate transaction. You're already motivated by the equity savings and the practical benefits of selling by owner this book shows you how to get organized and what professionals to enlist to help you through every step of the process.

"While the idea of selling your own home seems like a complicated endeavor the one thing I did know was that I was not without resources. There were lots of people and lots of places where I could get answers to questions. By questioning my lawyer I could get answers about legal things, answers about contracts, questions about financing, I could go to a local banker, appraisers can help. There are a number of resources you can tap into to get help.

You are not alone when selling your home on your own!"-- Pat Burds

Chapter 2

Setting the Correct Price
on Your Home

Setting the correct asking price for your home is the most important step in the process of selling your own home. Determining an accurate and fair asking price requires a little research and effort on your part, and help from a professional real estate appraiser. To appraise real estate means to estimate its value. In general, the goal of an appraisal is to provide an estimate of the market value of the property. Market value is the highest price that a property will bring in an open and competitive market. Using both the information you've gathered and the experienced, professional opinion of your appraiser will help ensure that the price you've set is reasonable and consistent for a property like yours within your real estate market.

Competitive advantage of selling by owner and appraisals

The most common error for-sale-by-owner homesellers make is overpricing their property based on nothing more than wishful thinking and emotion. Always remember that a major advantage of selling by owner is that you can afford to be more price-competitive compared to similar agent-listed properties and still preserve more of your equity. Don't shoot yourself in the foot by setting an asking price that is the same or more than comparable agent-listed properties. Buyers do their research too, and very few are willing to pay more for a property than they need to. Retain the competitive advantage you have selling by owner by pricing your home realistically.

The dilemma faced by you in pricing your home is simple: overprice it and it won't sell; underprice it and you'll lose money. One fact to realize is that few buyers will show up with cash in hand and pay your asking price. Most buyers must obtain financing to buy a home and here is where a safeguard against the buyer paying too much is embedded. Most lenders will not issue a mortgage for more than a specific percentage (typically 80-95%) of the appraised value of the property. Therefore, it is very important to know the current appraised value of your property when setting your asking price.

It's important that you not waste your time trying to sell an overpriced home it will be difficult, if not impossible to sell: especially in a tough buyer's market. Setting the correct price will help sell your home faster because knowledgeable buyers won't make offers on overpriced homes. If your house sits on the market for an extended period, buyers will buy other fairly priced homes and when you do eventually lower your price now your home is stale making it even more difficult to sell. *Buyers are more likely to make a reasonable offer on a reasonably priced home, and are likely to make no offer at all on an overpriced home.*

GET AN APPRAISAL, if you don't already have one. An appraisal generates an accurate dollar value for your property by an expert trained in determining the value of homes. An appraisal enables you to know your bottom line, and if necessary during the negotiations, you can produce the appraisal documents and demonstrate to the buyer that the house is accurately and fairly priced. Some appraisers offer a service specifically for for-sale-by-owners where they simply do a "mini-appraisal" or "appraisal update." These appraisals include site inspections and comparables and are similar to those performed for home-equity loans or refinances. With these modified services the appraiser will give you what you need and want - a fair and accurate price to ask for your home. This service is usually much cheaper than a full-scale appraisal, and can be done faster. So ask your appraiser.

What is an appraisal?

An appraisal consists of a written, formal estimate or opinion of value as determined by a state-certified and trained appraiser. The two most well-known professional associations of appraisers are the American Institute of Real Estate Appraisers and the Society of Real Estate Appraisers. Select an appraiser that you feel comfortable with. Get recommendations from friends and neighbors. Ask about experience, the more experience the better. Ask for recommendations -what banks and mortgage companies are they approved to do work for? Satisfactory answers to these questions will foster your confidence in the appraiser and in the dollar value they attach to your property.

The most common method used to establish the market value of a property for residential real estate is the direct sales comparison (or market comparision) approach. An estimate of value of obtained by comparing the subject property (your property) with recently sold properties that are similar to yours (comparables). The appraisal itself typically consists of two components: a site inspection of the property, followed by a thorough, parametric market analysis that compare similar properties to the subject property (your house).

Step 1: Site inspection

The first step that's taken during an appraisal is to determine the size of the home (square footage).

How to measure square footage: Measure all 4 sides as measured outside. For a rectangular house the formula is simply length multiplied by width = square footage. If the house is irregular in shape it's slightly more complicated. Don't simply add up the square footage of each individual room to get the total size; this is incorrect and will result in a smaller measured size. This is not a minor consideration. An appraiser with 20 years experience recently said at a homeselling seminar that "the measurement of a home is a significant part of the appraisal and frequently it is incorrect! Up to 50% of the real estate agents' or brokers' listing sheets are incorrect with regard to square footage". In other words, most homeowners don't know the correct size of their homes therefore they can't know what the correct price is either. In many cases this error doesn't amount to much, although some measurement errors can mean a $3,000 to $6,000 dollar difference in appraised value. The largest difference this appraiser has seen due to inaccurate measurement is $25,000. That means that the real estate agent *underpriced* the home by $25,000 because of not understanding how to measure square footage.

Step 2: Market analysis

The market analysis constitutes the bulk of the work of an appraisal. The appraiser will compare your property with other similar homes that have recently sold (< 6 months). Since no two parcels of real estate are ever exactly alike, each comparable property must be compared to the subject property and sales price must be adjusted for any dissimilar features and qualities. The main factors that require adjustments are grouped into four categories:

Date of sale: an adjustment may be made if economic changes occured between the date of sale of comparable properties and the appraisal date.

Location: Adjustments may be necessary for differences in location. Properties might differ in price from neighborhood to neighborhood, and even among locations in a neighborhood.

Physical features: Age of the building, lot size, construction quality, landscaping, square footage, general condition, garages, and fireplaces are features that must be similar or adjustments may be required.

Terms and conditions of the sale: These can become important if the sale is not financed by standard mortgage procedures. For example, if the seller finances part of the sale in exchange for a higher sales price this could affect the overall analysis.

So a market comparison is simply a determination of comparable worth. The appraiser will use the sales prices (not asking prices) of homes similar to yours to determine the value of your home on the market. A minimum of 3 comparables is required.

Similarities used in selecting comparables

The key to an accurate appraisal is in the methodological collection of information. The appraisal process involves specific procedures to collect and analyze this information in order to arrive at a determination of market value. This information is divided into two classes:

1. Specific information covering the details of the subject property as well as comparative data of similar properties.

2. General data covering the economic climate of the region, general information about the region, city and neighborhood. Of particular importance is the neighborhood, where an appraiser identifies the physical, economic, social and political influences that directly affect the value of your property.

The following areas will be evaluated in an appraisal to determine market value.

1. Style of home; compare capes with capes
2. Roughly the same square footage
3. Same area of town (ideally the same neighborhood)
4. Same number of bedrooms and baths
5. Roughly the same amenities; compare homes with fireplaces to homes with fireplaces; pool homes with pool homes, etc.)

Appraisals are based on many things, including comparables. Comparables are houses in your immediate neighborhood that have a comparable number of bathrooms, bedrooms, and kitchen appliances, similar heating, air conditioning and landscaping, etc. Appraisers look at the most recent sales prices of three such homes to establish the current value of your house. Comparables are key elements in their calculations. It's never easy to price your own house because of your skewed opinion about its individuality. However, if you have made a lot of improvements in the past two years, getting comparables in this market may not do justice to your home's value.

If you are in the early stages of considering selling, you may benefit from inspecting the appraisal that was done on your current home when you purchased it. Simply ask for a copy of your home's appraisal from your mortgage lender and, according to law the company must comply. You can learn a lot from your appraisal.

Neighborhood Information: The following is a listing of the type of information that would be available about your neighborhood:

1. The location: urban, suburban or rural?
2. How built up: over 75 percent, 25 - 75 percent, under 25 percent?
3. Growth rate: rapid, stable, slow?
4. Property values: increasing, stable, declining?
5. Demand/supply: shortage, in balance, oversupply?
6. Marketing time: under three months, three to six months, over six months?
7. Present land use: single family, two-to-four family, multi-family, commercial?
8. Land use change: not likely, likely, in process?
9. Predominant occupancy: owner, tenant, vacant (0 - 5%), vacant (over 5%)?
10. Single-family house price range: low, high, predominant?

Here are some aspects of the neighborhood that will be rated on an appraisal report: Good, Average, Fair or Poor.

11. Employment stability.
12. Convenience to employment.
13. Convenience to shopping.
14. Convenience to schools.
15. Adequacy of public transportation.
16. Recreation facilities.
17. Adequacy of utilities.
18. Property compatibility.
19. Protection from detrimental condition.

20. Police and fire protection.
21. General appearance of properties.
22. Appeal to market.

What about your neighborhood? By reading your appraisal, you can find out what components of your house and neighborhood are valuable and quantify their value. How much does the second bath add to the value of the house? How much does the lack of central air conditioning detract from the value of the house?

It's important to remember that appraisers don't set prices. They document current market conditions and try to predict what a given home will sell for. Appraisers try to show on paper what other similar sellers have done as a guide for attaching a dollar amount to a property. A good appraisal is as close to an objective evaluation as you can get. But also remember that appraisals do have an element of subjectivity, especially when it comes to the selection of what a comparable property is, so read your appraisal and make sure you agree with what it says. Appraisals can be changed.

Points to consider when setting your price

1. Your buyer will want to be sure your price is consistent with the market. Show them the appraisal or your market research of comparable homes that recently sold in your area and demonstrate that the price is fair. If you've priced your property at a premium because of your specific situation, be prepared to provide convincing evidence to justify the higher price. For example, you may have just learned that a major employer is expanding which should drive up the prices of homes like yours.

Also be aware that in many major cities new interactive Home Price Information Services are available that allow the caller to learn the selling prices of any recently sold home in a specific region. Smart buyers will find out what you paid for your home, examine the recent selling prices of comparable homes in the neighborhood, and be well informed about what you should be asking before they call for an appointment.

2. Demonstrate to the buyers that they save money because no sales commissions are involved, and you net more money for the same reason. The following example illustrates the dollars and sense of a by owner transaction for both you and your buyer.

	Broker	**By Owner**
Appraised Value	**$100,000**	**$100,000**
Asking Price	**$106,000**	**$103,000**
Sales Price	**$103,000**	**$100,000**
Owner's Net	**$96,820**	**$100,000**

Assumptions: House appraises at $100,000 and buyer negotiates price downward by $3,000 in both cases. Selling by owner: Buyer saves $3,000 and seller avoids paying $3,180.

Using a broker requires that either the buyer, the seller or both pay the commission. If the buyer pays asking price, they pay the commission. If the buyer downwardly negotiates the selling price below appraised value, the seller pays the commission. Downward negotiation costs the buyer and seller proportionate amounts. Eliminating the broker saves $6,180 in commission: The buyer saves $3,000 and the seller avoids $3,180 in this example. In a buyer's market, it is reasonable to expect the buyer to save proportionately more money, whereas in a seller's market the seller will save more.

Sales Tax Analogy: Another way to explain to the buyer how they save by purchasing from you is a sales tax analogy. A sales tax is usually tacked on to an item's selling price. The merchant or seller collects the tax from the buyer and passes the tax along to the state. Similarly, a real estate commission is tacked on to the sales price of the property. The funds to cover the tax originate from the buyer's pocket, flow through the homeseller and land in the real estate agent's pocket! Thinking about a real estate commission as a tax can reinforce the idea that it's really the buyer who pays the commission when they buy a listed property, and why it's the buyer who *really* stands to benefit when purchasing directly from the owner!

"We dropped the price we had with the real estate agent by 6% because we figured were not going to lose that commission fee when selling it on our own. That made the price more attractive and our buyer didn't even want to negotiate price."-- Graciella Callas

Doing your own appraisal

You can do almost exactly what an appraiser would do when they calculate a property's value using the direct sales comparison approach. You would begin by gathering comparable sales information, which would be the final selling prices (not the asking prices) of properties like yours in your neighborhood. This information is obtained by visiting your county courthouse or clerks office and looking up the information in the recorder of deeds office. Use these prices of comparable homes as a basis for your asking price, then adjust them by the value of the differences between the sold homes and your home to arrive at your price. The asking price will probably be inflated somewhat to allow for some "downward negotiation" that most buyers expect. How much cushion to put into your price depends on your specific needs and situation. A good rule of thumb is to set your asking price 1-3% or more above your bottom line to allow for some negotiation and to cover the costs of a buyer coming to you through a "buyers broker."

Also if you have available the computer service where you can simply call up and get the selling prices of homes, this is an efficient way to gather comparative data.

"I went down to city hall and took a look at the prices that the lots on either side of us sold for, and the fact that we had put a considerable amount of money into the property to finish it off (it was a new construction). We knew what we paid for it and we didn't want to go below that number." -- Pat Burds

Real estate agent "appraisals" & real appraisals

In theory, agent-generated prices should be close to professionally appraised value. However, real estate agents are not valid real estate appraisers, as evidenced by the fact that banks do not lend money based on the value attached to a home by a real estate agent! Mistakes like mis-measuring the square footage of the home translates into inaccurate prices being attached to homes. Protect yourself and get an appraisal done by a professional appraiser.

Another reason not to use real estate agent comparative market analyses is that you may have to second-guess the accuracy of the amount the agent has attached to your home. Consider the motivations of the agent giving you the market analysis: First, they want to list your home and second, they want it to sell. Some real estate agents behave as if these are conflicting and competing goals. Some agents will inflate the value of your home in an effort to win the listing: after all, if Agent X says they can get you $10,000 more than Agent Y, you might be seduced by Agent X. After the honeymoon is over, you've listed and no buyers are looking at your home, the agent will probably tell you that "you have overpriced your home and will need to drop the price to sell it!" These games will only frustrate you, and cost you thousands of dollars in the end. Save yourself the expense and headache, spring for the professional appraisal right from the start. You'll be glad you did!

Remember, real estate agents are not professional real estate appraisers...banks or mortgage companies do not, and will not, lend money based on the dollar value resulting from an agent's market analysis. In other words, real estate agent market analyses are relatively worthless because the veracity of the value is uncontrolled...*lenders know it and now you know it!*

Pricing above fair market value

You could get lucky and find a cash-rich buyer to purchase your home above its appraised value, but don't count on it! Buyers are smart, they're immersed in the market, they've seen lots of properties and probably know the reasonable price-ranges for properties they're interested in. In fact, if your strategy is to inflate your price substantially to see if anyone bites, thinking that you can always lower your price later, think again-the only one to get bitten will be you. Buyers are more likely to make a reasonable offer on a reasonably priced home, and are likely to make no offer at all on an overpriced home. Overpricing your home will generate no offers, no negotiation, no sale.

Also, most buyers will be advised by their attorney to make their offer to buy your home contingent upon whether the home's selling price is at or below the appraised value. If you know the appraised value before-hand, you won't have to sweat out the appraisal after a contract is signed and your home is off the market. If this contingency is not met (your property appraises for less than the selling price, you need to lower the price, re-negotiate the deal, or lose the sale!). So get an appraisal, or appraisal update.

Pricing your home knowing its appraised value

Here is where a combination of both *art* and *science* is necessary. The science is the objective dollar value generated by the professional ap-praisal. The art is in weighting that figure with your needs, your timetable, your knowledge of the local market, and your expectations concerning your prospective buyers' motivations and needs. Assuming you are not desperate to sell your home "tomorrow," a good rule of thumb is to set your asking price 3 - 5% or more above the appraised value as a starting point. This will give you some room to negotiate on price and should be realistic from a mortgage lender's point of view. If the market is slow, with lots of homes like yours for sale (a buyer's market), you may need to be more price com-petitive, pricing no more than the appraised value.

"When we arrived at our sales price we added an 8% cushion on the sales price to give us some room to negotiate, basically because every house deal has some negotiation, and we knew exactly what we needed to get out of the house, and we were prepared to go down the 8% from our asking price. But fortunately we got our asking price." -- Ben Hale

"My husband is more positive he wants to get more money for the house, while I tend to be more conservative. We consider the pieces of information we have about the house (appraisals, comparatives) and then we arrive at a price that allows for a little negotiation...and that seems to work well." --Jeannie St. Pierre

Advantages of a fairly-priced home offered by owner

An advantage to selling on your own is that you probably can sell it faster than you could with an agent, and net more money (or walk-away cash) at the closing. In fact, in some markets up to 60% of the properties listed with real estate agents do not sell; either the listing expires or the homeowner gets discouraged and takes the property off the market.

The following is from a brochure that advertises sales materials to real estate agents. This blurb below is intended to be read by real estate agents only...not homeowners! It's eye-opening that the real estate industry acknowledges its failures.

> Successful real estate professional invest in education, training and promotional material to expand their business. Consumer-directed videos are an emerging sales tool to help you increase your income.
> *"Expired Listing" 30-60% of all listings expire...a great source of potential business! This explanatory video covers the main reasons for expiration: Marketing, Condition and Price. Sellers learn how to analyze and improve each of these areas using your services. "Expired Listing" encourages them to list again...with you!"*

In fact, a large percentage of the homeowners who sell their own property actually did give agents a prior opportunity. But after 6 months or a year of frustration with listing agents the homeowner takes matters into their own hands, and gets the job done. Others decide to do it right the first time and sell it themselves.

Bottom line: Get a professional appraisal.

By now it should be clear that the more information you have about the real estate market in your area, the better off you will be as a seller. Don't underestimate the importance and value of a professional appraisal as a key step in pricing your home accurately and helping you avoid some of the pitfalls mentioned above. A fair and accurate price will speed the selling process by prompting more attractive offers and improve your negotiating position. Protect yourself and your equity and get a professional appraisal!

Chapter 3
Enhancing the Appearance
of Your Home

"I painted the trim. I looked for trouble spots and most of the work was
cosmetic in nature: touch-up painting, cleaning, simple stuff like that..."
--Ben Hale

The most important elements to successfully selling by owner is the
prior preparation of both yourself and your home—be an informed seller,
and you'll be more confident, and ultimately, more successful!

One of the first steps to becoming a confident homeseller is knowing that your home is in its very best condition - inside and out. Remember
that you are in a competition. Your home is competing with other similar
homes in your area for a limited number of buyers. Remember that buyers
will want to buy the home that best suits their needs, that is in the best

location, at the best price and yes, that looks the best. Selling by owner gives you a competitive edge on price compared to the competition (agent-listed properties); make your home look as good or better than those higher-priced homes and you have eliminated your competition!

The secret to enhancing the appearance of most homes is simply paying attention to details. The strategy is to prevent the buyer's attention from being drawn away from the overall outstanding appearance of your home by a few flaws that could have been easily corrected. Remember the old saying that you only have one chance to make a good first impression. Do that deferred maintenence: replace the broken garage window, repair the torn screen in the side door, fix the leaky faucets. If it's truly a minor repair, fix it and be done with it! Always remember that buyers will want a home that is in "move-in" condition.

"As the seller, you need to come through the house and evaluate every-thing with a critical eye. Look around and always ask 'would I want to buy this place.' Keep things in perspective: you're selling a house here, not your children!" -- Pat Burds

Prior to trying to sell a home, many homeowners fix up the prop-erty by making minor repairs and alterations, thereby enhancing its appeal. Some homes need more involved repairs and maintenance, like painting and re-carpeting, to make them more saleable. The following suggestions assume that all the necessary major jobs have been done (inside/outside paint-ing, carpet replacement, etc.) prior to advertising your home for sale and that you feel ready to invite potential buyers into your home. It's important that absolutely everything in your home be in working order. Make all the nec-essary repairs so that your home will pass any inspection requested by a potential buyer before the first buyer comes to visit. Don't make the mis-take of thinking that the buyer will overlook some "minor" defects.

Take a tour of your home and evaluate its condition from the per-spective of a potential buyer. What can you do to overcome the weaknesses? What condition are the carpets in? Most people look at the floors or carpets almost immediately when they walk into a room. If your carpets are worn, damaged or in an out-of-date color, they may need replacement. Do the walls need a fresh coat of paint? What's the condition of the wallpaper?

These tasks can be a major undertaking, requiring substantial effort, planning and expense. But sometimes it's necessary to sell the property. And remember that you'll probably net more money by performing repairs before negotiating with the buyer because otherwise the buyer will want compensation that more than covers the expense of the repairs. Obviously, a home that is attractive and appeals to the buyer's eye will have a better chance of being purchased closer to your asking price.

You must take an objective look at the general condition of your property from a potential buyer's perspective. Concentrate on areas that need attention that will make your home look better: painting, replace worn tile or linoleum, replacing worn carpeting. If the exterior paint is faded and chipping, you need to repaint. It will be less expensive for you to have it painted than giving a cash re-painting allowance the buyer. To pick the color go to some new developments and see what the local builders are using— these are the popular contemporary colors (choose the one that best complements your home). The same suggestion goes for anything that needs repair or refurbishing. Any drawback, like a carpet that is worn-out and needs replacing, will stand out in the buyer's mind. What you consider a minor defect may be perceived as a fatal flaw by a potential buyer. Why would the buyer purchase a home that needs carpet when he can get a similar home with nice carpeting? That's the major risk involved in not fixing something— *the flaw impedes the sale of your home, you waste your time and marketing dollars, and don't sell.*

Obviously, a home that is attractive and appeals to the buyer's eye will have a better chance of being purchased. Remember that a good home SELLS ITSELF! All other things being equal, a clean, well-maintained home will sell faster and for a higher price than a comparable house that isn't as attractive.

Why it's important for the outside of your home to look its best

The Drive-by: Many buyers who are interested in your home will call you up and ask some questions about your home. If they like what they hear about your property some will want to schedule a viewing appointment, others will want the address so they can *"drive-by."* The request for the drive-by means that the buyers are interested but not quite sure if they want to personally inspect the property yet. The drive-by is a non-committal, non-threatening way for buyers to see the general appearance of your house, the yard and the neighborhood. Therefore, you must anticipate the drive-by and adequately prepare for it!

Inspect your home from the perspective of these potential buyers. Drive up from the street and view your home through the buyer's eyes. Is the yard and landscape well-maintained? Keep the lawn mowed, and add a dose of fertilizer to make it look especially healthy. Remember that from the buyer's perspective established lawns, trees and gardens are advantages that existing homes have over new constructions. Pick up clutter from the yard and keep the lawn neat. Park your vehicles in the garage, around the corner or around the street so that the view of your home is uncluttered and unobstructed.

Trace the path that the buyer will take to get into the house. Is the walk well-maintained. What will the buyer see? Clean or fix things that need attention. Get dead branches and leaves off the roof and out of the gutters. Pull the weeds in the sidewalk, get rid of dead bushes, trim the shrubs, paint the rusty stair railing and clean or replace the front door mat. These fix-ups are relatively easy and inexpensive, and will help pique the buyer's interest.

"We did a little bit of touch-up painting and I augmented some of the landscaping outside with some lattice work underneath the front steps..." -- Pat Burds

Finally, look at your front door. What condition is it in? Is it nice-looking and well-maintained, or is it scuff-marked, with faulty knobs and locks? The front door can be symbolic of what's inside. Fix the door so that it accurately reflects the quality of your home, and preserve that good first impression. Spruce up the entryway to make it as inviting as possible. Get a new welcome mat. Keep house and yard lights on during the early evening hours so that drive-bys can see the home.

One last thought on the exterior: get a second opinion. Ask someone whose opinion you value what their overall impression of your place is from the outside, and what could be done to improve it. A fresh set of eyes can be very insightful.

Landscaping to increase appeal

A well-maintained exterior will be a positive reflection on the overall condition of your property, both inside and out. Here are a few suggestions that will entice drive-by lookers to get out of the car and see more.

1. Keep the grass mowed. Fertilize it regularly so that it looks its best.
2. Edge between your lawn, driveway and walkways.
3. Remove dead leaves, branches and grass clippings from the lawn.
4. Trim trees and hedges. Prune evergreens and shrubs.
5. Put new mulch around trees and shrubs.
6. Put away lawn mowers and gardening tools.
7. Weed and cultivate flower beds/gardens.

8. Make sure that the exterior paint is in good condition.

9. Keep gutters and rainspouts in good condition.

10. Repair fences and gates; paint if necessary.

11. Hang baskets of flowers and plants create a homey feeling.

12. Hose down the driveway, remove oil stains and recoat if necessary.

Simple ways to enhance the interior of your home

When preparing the interior of your home for sale, keep a simple rule in mind: Increase the clean, reduce the clutter, and create a welcoming, homey feeling.

CLEAN: Stand in the corner of your living room and take a look around. How does it look? If you feel the room is nice, fresh and clean, you're all set. If not, determine where there is room for improvement. Make everything clean and spotless. Does the carpet look dirty and worn. Sometimes a good shampooing will bring a carpet back to life. Carpets that are threadbare, with worn spots will not be an asset to your home. Replace them. Are the walls clean and free of smudges, or can you see the kids' handprints on them? Clean the walls, or re-paint if necessary. Clean out the fireplace if you're not using it. The house must be clean or you can't sell it.

"I took Windex to everything; the counters, the sink and, of course, the windows - it sparkled!" -- Pat Burds

CLUTTER: Buyers like homes that are neat as well as clean. Pick-up the clutter and pack it away. The objective is to present the room in its best light. If a room is too cluttered with knickknacks or collections, or if there is too much furniture so that it is difficult to see the room, the buyer is likely to be distracted by the details (the clutter, furniture) and is less likely to evaluate the qualities of the room itself. So rather than remembering the nice woodwork in the room or the strategic positioning of the fireplace, the buyer remembers your beer can collection or thimble collection and retains a less than ideal memory of what that room had to offer. Don't allow your personal belongings to distract attention from the room. Make an effort to remove anything that could make a buyer feel uncomfortable, such as religious or political items, or objects of questionable taste. For example, maybe the moosehead over the fireplace would be upsetting to some buyers. Who knows, maybe they're Bullwinkle fans. Why risk losing a sale because you're a hunter and, by chance, the prospective buyers object to hunting. Hunting has nothing to do with a real estate transaction; however, if buyers feel uncomfortable, for even the silliest reason, they won't make an offer.

Again, you will benefit from inviting a second opinion about the appearance of a room from a trusted friend. The goal is to make the home ready to accept a new owner by making it as inviting as possible; the less the home reflects the fact that you live there, the easier it will be for the buyers to imagine themselves living there.

Remove clutter from the floor, secure throw rugs etc,,and make sure that there is nothing buyers can trip over when viewing your home. You may be liable for any injuries.

FEELING: When a buyer enters your home, you want them to feel "at home." This feeling can be instilled through all of their senses. They see the size, the shape and color scheme of each room; they feel the temperature of the room; they smell the air; listen to the sounds; they feel the textures of the flooring and the effects of proper lighting. Luckily for you, most of these elements are at least partially under your control. A clean, clutter-free home is an ideal context for a buyer to feel at home, and to seriously consider purchasing

your home. We'll give some tips and suggestions on how to create the most desirable atmosphere you can for each buyer who visits your home in Chapter 5: Showing your home to buyers.

Appliance warranties & repair records

As you're going through the house, you'll probably come across various warranties to appliances, service records, operating manuals etc. Gather up all of these documents into a folder and have them available for prospective buyers to inspect. While you're at it, gather up last year's utility receipts, (i.e. heating, cooling, water, electric) and property tax bills. Put them in a separate folder. It's also helpful to compute monthly averages of expenses so that you can answer these questions when the buyer asks. Having everything accessible and organized will give the buyer confidence that you know what you're doing, and that will translate into increased confidence in your property.

Regarding objects that do not stay: If you are taking the family heirloom chandelier in the dining room, remove it now and replace it with a suitable substitute. You can be assured that any fixture you do not want included in the sale will be all the more desired by the buyer. So remove those items before buyers visit, or label them conspiciously as not conveying or going with the property, and save yourself a headache down the road.

Major renovations and remodeling

If your home needs major repairs and renovations to sell it, you can either offer it as a "fixer-upper" and price it accordingly, or you can invest in the renovations for now and the future. Some properties, simply will not sell unless they are presentable, and in move-in condition, so major renovations are a necessity not an option.

If you intend to sell in the near future, there are some modifications that can be made not only to increase the salability of your property in the future, but also enhance your enjoyment of your home while you're still living there. There are many cost-effective improvements that you can make to your home that will increase it's livability and eventual market appeal. For example, investing in professional landscaping can pay off by increasing curb-appeal to bring in buyers. If you remodel your kitchen, you'll be able to enjoy it and most likely get back 100 percent of your investment when you do sell. The same applies for an additional bathroom. The chart below gives some general costs and expected returns on some renovations when the home is sold less than one year later. Keep in mind that these are national averages...so your mileage may vary.

REMODELING YOUR HOME: COST VS. RESALE VALUE

Job	Cost	Value at Resale	Cost Recouped*
Master suite	$27,055	$24,744	91%
Major kitchen remodel	$17,170	$16,270	95%
Minor kitchen remodel	$5,835	$6,042	104%
Bathroom addition	$9,205	$9,046	99%
Bathroom remodel	$6,443	$5,292	82%
Family-room addition	$27,221	$24,019	89%
Deck addition	$6,620	$4,782	72%
Home office addition	$8,114	$4,801	59%
Two-story addition	$50,596	$42,438	84%

* If house is sold within one year after completion of remodeling project

SOURCE: REMODELING magazine October 1997

Some improvements may increase the perceived value of your home but not its actual market value. For example, the addition of a swimming pool most likely will not increase the value of your home when it's time to sell. However, if you love to swim consider the cost as money spent, not invested.

One final point to keep in mind when evaluating the decision to re-model is the relative position of your home's value within your neighbor-hood. Remember that the mechanics of the appraisal process require the accurate use of comparably featured properties for an accurate determina-tion of fair market value. If your house is already 20% or more valuable than other houses in your neighborhood, it may be difficult for an appriaser to justify attaching a much higher price tag to your home because of a few substantial improvements.

While the big decisions rest with you alone, it should be reassuring to you that there are resources you can consult at each step of this homeselling process to help you gather the best information for these decisions. In the previous chapter, the importance of a professional appraiser and the role that the appraisal plays in your pricing strategy was discussed. In this chapter we discussed the importance of getting your home in "move-in" condition, because this is want the buyer wants. It's critical for you because if you give the buyer what they want, they'll be much more likely to give you what you want- a sale!

You must apply this information to your specific situation and make adjustments when necessary. This strategy will help ensure that the information works best for you.

"There was a reason why I bought this house a few years ago. All I tried to do was get the place in optimum condition so that the home would have the best chance of selling itself." -- Pat Burds

Fix-up, clean-up checklist

The following table lists the areas and systems in your home that should be examined before you place the property on the market.

Windows:
> Sparkling windows are an indication that your home is well-maintained. Throughly clean the windows, and vacuum out the dead bugs and dust.

Kitchens:
> Clear off unused appliances from counters make them look spacious.
> Clean other appliances.
> Remove clutter from refrigerator door.
> Clean exhaust fan so there's no grease.

Bathrooms:
> Clear off vanity/sink, clean and sparkling.
> Remove mold/mildew in bathtub or on tile. Keep grout clean & white.
> Check condition of paint/wallpaper.
> Remove cat litterbox.
> Keep lid on toilet closed.

Bedrooms:
> Clean, reduce clutter.
> Clean out closets to the extent you can; keep the doors closed.

Attic:
> Check underside of roof for leaks.
> Clean and clear ventilation openings.
> Clean out stored junk.

Basement:
> Check for signs of wetness, cracked walls, damaged floors.
> Check for plumbing leaks.
> Clean out junk.

Windows and Doors:
> Wash windows.
> Check for smooth operation of all doors and windows.

Floors:
> Repair damaged regions.
> Clean baseboards and moldings.
> Check for loose or unstable handrails, posts etc. on stairways.

Electrical System:
> Look for signs of wear or damage.
> Repair broken switches and outlets; clean switchplates.
> Label circuits and fuses.

Plumbing:
> Clear slow-running drains.
> Fix leaky faucets.

Heating & Cooling Systems:
> Check or change furnace or air-conditioning filters.
> Clear area around furnace/air-conditioner.
> Have system serviced, if needed.

Chapter 4
Advertising and Marketing
Your Own Home

It's important to realize that when selling by owner you are responsible for advertising and marketing your home to the buying public. Your attractive home will sell itself, but only if buyers know it's for sale. Buyers need to be aware that your home is for sale and they need some basic information about it to make an informed decision whether it suits their needs. Ideally, you would identify *the* buyer most interested in your home, tell them its for sale and that would be it, *sold*. The catch is effectively locating that one perfect buyer. You know they're out there, but how do you find them? The answer is to advertise.

Target marketing

The objective of advertising is to target market your home to only those buyers truly interested in it, and motivate them to personally inspect your home. To achieve this goal you need an advertising and marketing plan. Each plan will be different depending on the resources in your area and how much money you are ready, willing and able to spend. We will give you the elements of a good plan shortly. However, be aware that good, effective advertising is not cheap. You may spend $500 - $1000, or possibly more on advertising, depending on how long it takes to sell, and the methods you select to advertise. It may be of some comfort to you to compare these up-front, out-of-pocket costs with the thousands of dollars you'll save on a real estate commission when you do sell.

"If you're going to pay a realtor $15,000, you have a lot of advertising there. If you look at it that way, you say this much money to advertise a month, and we started thinking...how long would it take us to get to $15,000....quite a while!" -- Jeannie St. Pierre

Advertising methods

In general, the more information about your home that is contained in your advertising and the more people exposed to that information, the better the ad will work for you. A sign in the front yard of your home is one of the most important and cost-effective means of advertising available to you. A sign lets passersby know that your home is for sale. And, if by chance a ready, willing and able buyer passes by, you may have the opportunity for a sale. However, if you're like most sellers, you want to sell your home reasonably quickly. To best accomplish this objective, you should maximize the exposure of your home to the buying public by using a variety of integrated and complementary advertising methods. In other words, you'll want to cover as many bases as possible. And keep in mind that a homeowner's marketing plan can be as unique as the home itself. There is no single, correct, formula to follow.

To effectively advertise your property you'll need a plan. Since you're responsible for getting the word out you have a few decisions to make early in the process:

☞ Determine an advertising budget

☞ Research the available advertising media in your area

☞ Decide on the right mix to sell your home

Determine a budget

When creating a marketing plan for your home, perhaps the best place to start is to take a look at your checkbook. Effective advertising doesn't have to cost a fortune, but it is still an investment. Get the facts about advertising alternatives available to you, and their costs, and develop realistic expectations and you will know what to expect. These costs will be less disruptive to the family budget if you plan ahead and earmark money for these costs. A common mistake that homeowners make is to commit too little money to advertising their home because they:

1) underestimate the costs of advertising and/or
2) underestimate the time period required to sell.

Don't make the mistake of underestimating this relatively minor up-front cost (compared to a full real estate sales commission).

The most important aspect of budgeting is planning for costs over time. If you sell quickly— great, you save some advertising money. Don't spend all of your advertising budget in the first few weeks, when you may have to advertise your property for three months or more. This is important. Plan for costs over time. Don't quit too soon because it will just waste your money and you'll prevent yourself from succeeding. This would be unfortunate because a sale could have been just around the corner!

Researching advertising alternatives

There are several effective advertising methods available to homeowners in many parts of the country. It is important for you to find out what each costs in your area. Be sure to ask about any frequency discounts and special plans that may be available. The primary options you have available to advertise your property are yard signs, classified ads, photo classified ads, for sale by owner publications, the Internet and open houses.

Yard signs

A sign in the yard is a good idea for most homesellers. First, it can attract drive-by house-hunters who like your neighborhood, but may not yet know your home is for sale. One popular method buyers use when searching for a new home is to simply drive around exploring neighborhoods. Buyers can get a reasonably complete and accurate picture of neighborhoods from the quality and style of homes, the residents, proximity to shopping, schools, transportation, recreational facilities etc. Second, a yard sign can provide a source of "word-of-mouth" advertising through anyone who sees it. And the yard sign serves as a landmark for potential buyers when they drive-by or when they visit. Obviously, a sign will work better if you live along a street with a substantial amount of traffic than if you live at the end of a cul-de-sac, or out on an isolated country road.

"We tried to sell our home with an agent for 6 months before deciding to sell on our own. We were amazed that we sold it ourselves within a week, just from a sign". -- Graciella Callas

How effective is a sign? According to a recent *USA Today* survey of homebuyers, 49% reported that they initially located the home they eventually bought just by seeing a sign in the yard! Another survey by Peartree Home Marketing Consultants in Toronto, Canada, found that better than 70% of people buying a home are introduced to it from a lawn sign from which they write down the telephone number. Clearly, if your for-sale-by-owner sign is in the yard, you'll get the calls directly from buyers who see the sign. Whereas properties listed with real estate agencies have the agency's telephone number; they get the calls and access to the buyers.

Since many buyers would prefer not to deal with agents, the sign placed in the yard of a home offered for-sale-by-owner is much more effective because potential buyers will actually call. Why don't buyers call on agent signs? One reason is to avoid a high-pressure sales pitch for that house or any others that the agent may have listed. Most people don't like to be "sold" something; they would prefer to search at their own pace and control the process. If buyers like what they see of your house, they will call for more information.

What should your sign be like? First a word on what types of signs to avoid. Don't use one of those cheap black and red signs you get in the hardware store. Signs like these may have potential buyers asking themselves, "did that sign say 'For Sale' or 'Beware of the Dog?'" Signs like these are too small and difficult to read. They detract from the otherwise attractive appearance of your home. Furthermore, bad signs can turn-off potential buyers because if you won't put a decent sign on your property how serious can you really be about selling? Always examine your behavior from the perspective of a potential buyer, and evaluate its impact on their desire to buy your property.

Ineffective sign

Characteristics of an effective sign

An ideal sign will look professional and attractive, complementing your attractive property. It will be easy to read and provide important information. Get a professionally made sign, that is large (18" x 24") with big, easy-to-read lettering on both sides. On the top of the sign let people know

HOUSE FOR SALE
By Owner
985-9403

BY APPOINTMENT ONLY

it's for sale. Put "House for Sale by Owner" or "For Sale by Owner" on the top in big letters. Remember that the phrase "by owner" is a potent selling point with buyers. Next, put your telephone number on the sign in large, clear easy-to-read numbers. You may also want to put "By Appointment Only" if you want time to prepare before showings, or want to discourage buyers from just dropping-in. Place the sign in a strategic position in the yard so that traffic on both sides of the street can easily see it, if possible. Also, if you live embedded in a large development or "off the beaten path", directional signs that tell buyers that there is a house for sale in the vicinity are effective. Ideally, place the signs at each choice point along the way from the main road, and direct the buyers right to their new home.

You may also want to have Fact Sheets that provide more detailed information about your home available outside near your sign. Fact sheets are especially important for people driving by who are interested in your home but need more information before they will commit to a visit. A well-prepared fact sheet will answer lots of their questions and may help keep a buyer interested. Store the fact sheets in a weatherproof canister attached right to your sign. Tennis ball cans (the clear plastic variety) work well.

What to expect from the sign in the yard

Of course, you expect to get phone calls from buyers. This will happen, and we'll discuss how to effectively deal with bona-fide calls from buyers in Chapter 5. Also expect to get calls from your neighbors wanting to know "what are you asking?" This is normal curiosity from people who have a vested interest in knowing what you intend to sell your property for. Politely provide them with the information they request, and be tolerant understanding that you may have behaved similarly in the past. They're just gathering comparative market data.

It's important for you to realize who is calling and why because chances are your neighbors don't want to buy your property. Don't get discouraged when, after you first place the sign in the yard, you receive a flurry of calls asking the price and no one calls back. This is normal neighbor behavior. If, after your sign has been up for a few weeks, and you are still getting the same type of calls, i.e. ask the price and never call back, you may want to re-evaluate how you arrived at your asking price. See Chapter 2.

Recently we had a homeowner tell us an interesting story about the effectiveness of signs in selling homes. One method real estate agents try to sell homes is by "caravanning." This involves putting a bunch of "prospective buyers" in a van and dragging them around to the agency's listed properties, hoping that someone will buy one of the homes. The homeowner who told us this story said that she would see these vans drive by her house on a regular basis, until she put her own for-sale-by-owner sign outfront. Then, the agency vans disappeared. She observed that the real estate agents were now taking the long way around the block, entering and leaving the development from another, less convenient road. She said it looked as if the agent's didn't want their prospects to see her sign...and she was right!

We've heard many accounts of buyers looking with agents who end up purchasing a for-sale-by-owner property because they were fortunate enought to see the FSBO sign. It usually happens like this: buyers and their agent visit a listed property in the same neighborhood as a for-sale-by-owner. The buyer sees the sign, returns for a drive-by without the agent, calls the owner, buys the property. Here is an illustration of why it's important for your property to be priced competitively. Buyers looking at agent-listed properties are seeing inflated prices (the fair market value of the home plus the sales commission attached!) When these buyers inspect your property, they see a home of comparable or better quality... and a lower price. Which home would you buy?

A good, professionally-made sign is a very cost-effective way to advertise your home. It's always out front working for you, letting people know your home is FOR SALE.

"One of the first things we did after deciding to sell by owner was to get a nice, custom-made sign. It was very attractive and you could see the phone number on both sides. We sold from the sign. He saw the sign, called us and bought it. It was easy!" -- Graciella Callas

Print advertising

Classified ads

A good way to reach potential buyers who may not pass by your home and see your sign is through widely-distributed print advertising. A standard, 4-line classifed ad is a common way to reach buyers. People who are serious about finding a home will often scan the newspaper looking for new ads. Remember that buyers actively search out homes offered directly by the owner, so it's always in your best interest to highlight the fact that you are, indeed, selling by owner.

There are several alternatives available in newspaper advertising. The first type of print ad that we'll discuss is the classified ad in your local newspaper. Lots of people read the newspaper, and some of them may even be looking for a house. However, you must keep in mind that you are severely limited in how much information you can put into a classified ad, so it's important to make every word count.

This is the recipe for producing a good classified advertisement:

1. Let the buyer know your property is offered for sale by owner this gives your property a competitive advantage in the mind of the buyer.

2. Next include the price buyers usually search within a defined price range.

3. Give the general location of your home or the exact street address (e.g. hill section, downtown, etc). Buyers want to know where it is. If you put in your exact street address realize that buyers may see your ad, however they may not call you after they drive-by. Those that do call after driving by should be considered hot prospects be - cause they already like what they've seen.

4. Give the approximate size of your home. Specify the number of bedrooms and baths. Every buyer has specific requirements in mind.

5. Include the best selling feature. For example, terms like *remodeled, below appraisal, owner relocating, large yard, low taxes* are inducements.

6. Include your phone number.

With these suggestions in mind, the following is an example of a good classified ad:

> **BY OWNER 15 Maple St.**
> **$150,000. Colonial, Hill Section,**
> **4 BRs, 2 Baths, recently remodeled**
> **555-3645**

A classified ad reaches lots of people, but the amount of information contained in it is limited. While a detailed, specific ad should enable buyers to pre-screen themselves, you may find that you get a lot of inquiries from people who turn out not to be good prospects. That initial phone call may be the time to do a little pre-screening yourself. Don't hesitate to ask the caller if they have any special needs or desires, and be sure to mention any potential deal makers or breakers, such as the distance to the main road, or proximity to schools.

Classified ads are best used to generate interest in your property based on a few well-chosen words and phrases. Since they don't contain much information , use the ad as a means to prompt calls and then provide the details. Buyers may be less likely to get excited about your house if they only read about it in a classified. So if buyers call you from classified advertising you'll need to fill in the blanks. The objective is tell the buyer enough to get them interested in a drive-by or scheduling an appointment for a personal showing. From the buyer's perspective, inquiring about a home in the classifieds is much like a blind date. It sounds good but they don't know if its a good match until they actually visit and personally inspect the property. Your objective is to entice the buyer to visit, and let the home sell itself.

A drawback to classified ads is that they are relatively generic, and could be describing many homes in the same price range and geographic

59

location. A buyer who has been searching the classifieds for a period of time probably has been frustrated by reading an ad that described their "dream home" only to be disappointed when actually visiting the home. The more a buyer wastes time pursuing wrong leads in the classifieds, the less likely he is to continue searching them. Plus you'll get tired of having buyers coming through your house who, for whatever reason, just aren't right for it. Relying on classified ads alone could lead to buyers disappointed and sellers discouraged because of the continued generation of false hopes and accompanying disappointments.

When using classified ads check for any frequency discounts and special packages they may offer. But remember that classified ads get expensive. As a cost reference, a four-line classified ad running for 30 days in the *Burlington Free Press* is $223.00; over $372.00 in the *Boston Globe*, $840.00 in the *New York Times*, and $728.00 in the *Washington Post*.

Over the years homesellers have consistently reported that newspaper classified ads tend to attract bargain hunters and tire-kickers. Newspaper classifieds are similar to cheap-looking yards signs: they make a poor first-impression. Given the cost of these ads and their poor effectiveness, advertising in the newspaper classified should be low on your list of priorities.

"A local newspaper had the ability to run a classified ad of our home, and in my mind, that reaches a point of diminishing return after a short period of time, even after a week"--Pat Burds

Photo classified ads

Remember that more information is better. Placing a photo ad in the newspaper will probably work better than a simple four- line text classified. After all, a picture is worth a thousand words, and a thousand words in the classifieds would cost you thousands of dollars. A photo classified is a good way to get more information in the ad.

These ads will be expensive. However, the photograph may attract more readers and help make your ad stand out. Make sure the photograph is clear and not too dark. Place the text description of your home below the photograph. Below is an example of a classified ad with a photograph. Keep in mind that simply taking out a larger ad in the same medium may not translate into more interested buyers. It is likely that the same pool of buyers who saw your 4-line classified will also see your more expensive photo ad as well. Given the cost of these ads and their poor effectiveness, advertising in the newspaper photo classifieds should be low on your list of priorities.

Home For Sale by Owner. Spacious south-end cape in nice family neighborhood. 3 BR, 1-1/2 baths, LR w/ fireplace, landscaped. Asking $119,900. Call 439-2312.

Also, in addition to your regional paper consider local community papers for both classified and photo advertising; depending on the distribution and readership these could be both more effective and less expensive.

For-sale-by-owner real estate publications

In many parts of the nation specific advertising publications that feature property for sale by owner are available. These publications feature only homes offered for sale by owner. These publications are effective because they typically provide lots of information about the home, and since most of the homes for sale by owner in a given region are compiled into one source, it enables the buyer to effectively and efficiently view and investigate most of these homes at once. Advertising your property in a for-sale-by-owner publication is an example of effective *target marketing*.

"Magazines work because of the pictures. The pictures of the houses, pictures of the inside, different rooms. The buyer knows what they are coming to see."--Jeannie St. Pierre

$175,900   **Suzie & Bob**
Essex - 18 Meadow's Edge   985-6303
Charming 2100 sq. ft. Cape in immaculate condition! Open floor plan, delightful country kitchen, tasteful decor with beautiful, professional landscaping. Custom oversized deck with patio, brick walkway. Four bedrooms, 2 baths.Sunken family room with cathedral ceiling, wainscoting, brick hearth with "fireview" soapstone woodstove. Exposed hardwood beams in kitchen & dining rooms.

Above is an example of an ad layout from a for-sale-by-owner magazine. The format of this ad enables the buyer to see photographs of the home and get a feel for what this home has to offer. The extensive description also provides lots of detail for the buyer. This format is very successful because it allows the buyer to make informed decisions about whether to visit a given house. The more information contained in your advertising, the less likely you are to attract lookers and shoppers, and the more likely you are to attract "hot" leads and your future buyer.

For-sale-by-owner magazines are appearing all over the country to meet the advertising needs of homeowners selling their own property. If you have a local for-sale-by-owner publication seriously consider using it. It is the most cost-effective way to advertise your home. Most have extended distribution times (weeks or months compared to just a day in the newspaper) and most ad options include multiple photographs and extensive written descriptions. Moreover, most for-sale-by-owner publications provide a complete range of products and services that will help you sell by owner.

"In our experience, advertising in the newspaper did not bring a whole lot of prospective buyers. Our experience has been that the FSBO publication brings the buyers."-- Dominick St. Pierre

"The for-sale-by-owner magazine made all the difference to us, the presence of high quality photos, said, more in those pictures than you could with thousands of words in a newspaper And the price of a classified ad in the newspaper was more than we could afford"-- Pat Burds

POUGHKEEPSIE

Family home, 3 bedroom, 1 bath, waterview of Appletree Bay, beautiful backyard with spruce & fruit trees. Stone patio, garage, new furnace. Motivated seller, Owner relocating.

914-287-XXXX   **$145,000.**

WEST PORTLAND

Beautifully decorated 2400 sq. ft. home on nice landscaped lot. 4 bedrooms, 2 baths, family room, luxurious master bath & much more.OPEN HOUSE SUNDAYS, 1-4 PM.

CALL FOR APPT 708-697-XXXX

Open houses

An "open house" is a pre-determined day and time when you invite anyone interested in your home to personally inspect it. Open houses can be effective in bringing more potential buyers through your home because an open house can be less personally intimidating to buyers. In a open house situation, there is a diffusion of responsibility. This means that the buyer is just one of many, and can remain relatively anonymous. In other words, there is less social pressure on the buyer to personally interact with you. And it affords an easy solution to the situation in which a buyer knows your home isn't for them as soon as they enter it! With other people or other buyers around they can slip away, without informing you that your house doesn't fit their needs or receiving the grand tour just to be polite.

Unfortunately, this degree of anonymity can also encourage lookers, shoppers and other sellers who are just using the opportunity to see your home for comparision purposes only. Also, there are some people who just have nothing better to do than to visit open houses for decorating ideas or for the cookies. These groups of people tend to give open houses an unfavorable reputation, and fortunately, they are very rare.

Homes can and do sell from open houses. Open houses work best for for-sale-by-owners when they receive lots of interest from their advertising in a relatively short period of time. For example, some of our magazine advertisers receive dozens of calls from buyers all wanting to see the home "today!" Obviously, showing the home this many times in a short period of time can wear on you. What some people do is schedule an impromptu open house for the following weekend. For example, the buyers are told that there will be an open house on Saturday or Sunday from 1 - 4 pm and they are welcome. This plan works well for several reasons. First, it allows you to condense your showings into a shorter amount of time, saving you time and hassle. Secondly, and perhaps more importantly, buyers will see the other interested buyers inspecting your home during the open house. This situation creates demand for your home and may prompt a quick and attractive offer from one of the buyers. Most buyers want to avoid a bidding war, and this can work to your advantage.

You may also choose to schedule an open house and coordinate its advertisement with your for sale by owner magazine advertising. For example, including a line in your ad that says "Open House, June 12 & 19 from 1 - 4PM", will prompt prospective buyers to call for directions and more information. In the next chapter, we will show you how to prepare and what to have available for buyers when they inspect your home during an open house.

The internet

Another relatively recent development that could give you access to lots of buyers are specialized Internet world wide web sites. Many for sale by owner publications offer Internet exposure to their customers as part of their advertising packages. These sites are highly functional and effective for both buyers and sellers alike. The major benefit of internet sites managed by for sale by owner publications is their popularity and conceptual design devoted to for sale by owner real estate. The print publication primes usage of the web site in the local market. Local usage of a for-sale-by-owner real estate web site translates into success since over 85% of all buyers are classified as "local," coming from within a 20 mile radius of the property that is eventually purchased.

The power of the Internet is in its exposure of your property to many potential buyers both locally and world-wide within a very short period of time. Some sites can post your ad in as little as one-hour from receiving it. Internet advertising should be one high-tech component of your total advertising plan.

Where the buyers are

If you know where buyers interested in your neighborhood and home are likely to be located you will be more able to target your advertising specifically to these groups. Talk to neighbors who have recently moved into the development or complex, and observe whether any patterns exist. Are there trends in terms of place of employment, previous neighborhood, or out-of-towners? Depending on what you learn, it might be beneficial to place your feature sheets in specific companies or neighborhoods . Also, the major employers in your area may have relocation departments that facilitate and assist their employees being transferred out and relocated into the area. Getting your feature sheets into this department could end up in packages sent out to relocated employees or on company bulletin boards.

The right mix

Once you've done your homework about the available advertising methods in your area and developed a budget, you're ready to develop and implement a plan.

Start with the essentials.

1. A sign is a relatively inexpensive, one-time cost, so get a good sign.

2. Your local for sale by owner publication is very important.

One strategy that for-sale-by-owners use in their advertising is to link or piggy-back one form of advertising to another.   Some for sale by owner homesellers include the internet address of the for sale by owner web site in their other print advertising so that a link to more information can be obtained about their property than would be feasable in a typical newspaper classified ad. But remember to compare the costs and examine your budget. If you must choose between advertising in the classifieds or for-sale-by-owner publications, our experience is that FSBO publications outperform the classifieds in bringing the buyers.

To advertise your home you'll need to be realistic. Find out what it costs to advertise, psychologically prepare to spend some money on ads, develop a strategically sound mix of advertising for maximum exposure, and get ready for the phone to ring!

Chapter 5

Showing Your Home:
How to Interact with Buyers

You've made the commitment to sell your home yourself. You're confident about your price. You've fixed up, cleaned up and spruced up. You've developed a good marketing plan and have your ads in place. Any day you'll start to get interested buyers contacting you. Now what?

Simply stated, the objective when showing your home is to allow potential buyers the freedom to be able to imagine themselves actually living in your home. Remember that your HOME WILL SELL ITSELF. You shouldn't spend a lot of time talking to the buyer (let the buyers dream). If you talk too much, they will be paying attention to you and not falling in love with the charm and character of your home, and the idea of living there.

Showing your home is simple. What you need to do is schedule the appointment, let the buyer visit and inspect your home and be ready to answer questions. Here are some suggestions regarding each facet of the home-showing process, starting with the all-important initial contact with the buyer over the telephone. Since your initial contact with the buyer will most likely be over the phone, you need to be prepared the FIRST TIME it rings!

How to deal with buyers over the telephone

Your telephone is the major link for contact between your future buyer and you. Your advertising has your phone number listed for potential buyers to call, and they will. You must answer the phone. Believe it or not, there are people who will spend hundreds of dollars on an effective, first-class advertisement; then go away on vacation without even so much as an answering machine left to handle callers! Unless someone is always present at your house, you *need* an answering machine when selling your own home.

Answering machine messages

Some people do not like talking to machines - so they simply hang-up. To reduce the likelihood of losing a potential buyer, leave a specific message about the home being for sale that compels the buyer to leave a message. Remember that by-owner sales are exclusive and special; the buyer wants to see your home first, before it's sold to someone else. If your message says your home is for sale and you are actively scheduling appointments, the buyer has to act now or lose the opportunity. To encourage people to leave messages, set up your answering machine with a specific message about your home being for sale, mention any special features, and warmly urge them to leave their name and number. Here's an example of an effective message:

> Hello, you've reached the Wilson's. No one is available
> to take your call. Our home is for sale at $150,000.
> and we'd love to show it to you. The house is spacious,
> located in a great part of town and recently updated.
> Please leave your name and telephone number and we'll call you
> back as soon as possible to schedule an appointment to see it.

"One of the nicest things abouts selling it on our own was that we were in total control of the showing schedule. We did not have to leave the house in the morning and wonder if people were going to look at the house that day. We had an answering machine; people called; we called them back and we would set up a time at our mutual convenience." -- Ben Hale

Information to give and receive from buyers over the phone

Ideally, you are at home to field the call because you can answer any specific questions that the buyer may have. What should you do when a buyer calls? First of all, keep a pad of paper by the phone. For each inquiry try to get the caller's name and phone number. The telephone log template shown here is a good standard, and will help ensure that you get the information you need.

TELEPHONE LOG

Date and Time:

Name:

Address:

Phone Number:

How did you hear about our house?

Out-of-Town or Local?

Renting or Currently Own?

Current House Sold?

Family: Married   Children #

Desire Fact Sheet?
  Date Mailed?

Viewing Appointment (Date & Time)

Comments:

Follow-up call:

Obtaining this information may seem unimportant, but if you need to cancel or reschedule due to an emergency, you'll be glad you can call, instead of risking a sale by not being home for a scheduled appointment! Also, sometimes a buyer may have the best intentions, but simply does not show up for an appointment and is too embarrassed to call again. They will probably **never** call you again, so it's up to you to call them back and re-kindle their interest. You have a lot at stake here. If you have their number you can call and assure them that it is not too late to reschedule.

When a buyer calls the first time, you should ask where they heard about your home. This will help you track and evaluate the effectiveness of your advertising. Buyers may want you to describe the house to them over the phone. Be prepared. Before that first phone call comes in, think about your home's special assets and how you might try to describe them to someone who's never seen your home. Try to remember what attracted you to your home when you bought it, and recapture that excitement for the prospective buyer. You must be very positive about your home and be able to express its finer features.

When you begin to show your home you will need a fact sheet on hand for people who see your home. (We'll show you how to produce a great fact sheet soon.) Be prepared to cite some attractive features of the neighborhood/community; e.g. the school system was recently recognized as one of the best in the state, it's a nice quiet neighborhood, very friendly neighbors, etc.

Better yet, have your fact sheet handy by the phone so you'll remember to stress all the important aspects to each caller. If the caller hesitates, or is reluctant to schedule a visit, offer to mail your fact sheet to them. This step could re-ignite their interest after they see more information, and a picture of your place. Stamps are cheap.

Also, be prepared for the question, "So, why are you moving?" Don't get caught off guard. Consider whether your answer to that question could affect their interest in your home. For example, answers like "because we have outgrown this house; we have four children" or "the house is too big now that our children are grown" probably won't affect your position. However, if you say "because we don't like the neighborhood or neighbors" you may have some explaining to do. Think ahead, and anticipate the impact of what you say.

If the buyer wants to see more, schedule the appointment for them to visit. One final point: give good directions. Faulty directions on your part will upset your buyer and set a sour mood for the showing, if they show up at all.

"Selling your home yourself you must remember you now are a store owner. You own something and now you are trying to sell it, so that means you had better be open for business. If people call your store you make sure you answer the phone or call them back. If you don't have an answering machine, GET ONE! Get your messages off the machine and call them back"-- Pat Burds

TIP: Many telephone companies now offer inexpensive second-line services like "ring mate." The number is different but it rings on your line with a distinctive ring. This is convenient because the distinctive ring tells you it's a call about your property because the number is only published in your advertising.

Drop-ins

If someone knocks on your door unannounced and wants to see your home - use simple commonsense. There can be serious personal risks involved in letting unknown or unexpected people into your home. Here common sense should be used. You have a choice to make: They could be qualified buyers who just happened to be in the neighborhood and really want to see your home, or they could not be interested in buying at all. Get them to write down their name and phone number in the visitor book that you have specifically for prospective buyers. Legitimate buyers shouldn't balk at this. Also most people don't look at homes at night - tell them to come back tomorrow when they can see all the fine features of your home. Don't show your property if you are alone, particularly if you consider yourself vulnerable. Have a friend or relative present when you show the property. As a precaution, you might be careful by removing any portable valuables from each room, and keeping them in a safe place.

We've dealt with thousands of homeowners and we haven't heard any complaints of security problems from people selling their own homes.

What to have available for the showing

Once you've set that first appointment, you're on your way. If you're like most people you'll probably be a little nervous the first few times you show your house. This is normal. Keep in mind that you have a very valuable piece of property, an exclusive and special home that buyers highly desire. Be confident that you've done your best to prepare, and *let your home sell itself!*

Fact sheet

The fact sheet (also known as a feature sheet) provides most of the necessary information a buyer will want to know about your property, neighborhood and community. It should have a photo of the exterior (so that buyers can remember your home), the square footage of the home and lot size, number of bedrooms and bathrooms, room sizes, special features (den, family room, fireplace), property taxes, average monthly utility bills, names of school districts (elementary, secondary), ages of appliances, type of heat, water source. Also helpful is a narrative description of your home that will give these data life and character, distinguishing your home in the buyer's mind.

The following is a example for the layout of an effective fact sheet. The photograph on the top is a print, that you secure to the original. Simply have color copies of the original produced, or you can get reprints of the photo and mount a photograph on each feature sheet. For the best results, most for-sale-by-owner magazines can prepare your fact sheets with professional typesetting and design services for a reasonable cost. Their assistance will also ensure that your fact sheets are complete and professional looking.

For-Sale-by-Owner $128,900.

1234 Greenfield Road

This home has been recently updated and well-maintained. It has a lovely yard, consisting of 2 acres of professionally landscaped lawns and established perennial gardens including a stone wall and lots of mature maple and oak trees. This home is located in a great family neighborhood with an outstanding school system.

* 2200 SQUARE FEET
* 4 BEDROOMS
* 2-1/2 BATHS
* FIREPLACED MASTER SUITE HAS 3/4 BATH W/ JACUZZI
* FAMILY ROOM W/ FIREPLACE
* LARGE KITCHEN W/ ATRIUM DOORS
* DINING ROOM W/ WINDOW SEAT
* GAS HOT WATER HEAT

* MAPLE HARDWOOD FLOORS
* TWO-CAR GARAGE
* PAVED DRIVEWAY

* FINISHED BASEMENT
* FULL ATTIC
* LARGE CLOSETS
* DRILLED WELL

This home is well-insulated and energy-efficient. Average gas and electric is $85 / month. Taxes $2,200. The Davidson school district was a 1992 National Education Association Blue Ribbon winner (Best in state.) Items staying with property: Swing set, jungle gym, woodstove in living room. Items not staying: curtains, chandelier in dining room. Washer and dryer negotiable.

BOB AND SUE JACKSON 555-1234

A good fact sheet will contain the information and features about the property so that the buyers have a convenient "take-home" message about your home. When they discuss the relative merits of your home later, your home will be top-of-mind because the fact sheet will refresh their memory. Also, since you've designed the fact sheet, you can emphasize the positives, and diminish the impact of any negative features they may have noticed .

"I need to look at this home with the eye of a buyer. A few years ago, I walked through this house and there were reasons why I wanted to buy it. Now I have to have that attitude for people who are going to walk through that door...Why would somebody want to buy this house? This meant doing things beyond just the clean-up, paint-up, fix-up; it meant knowing the neighborhood, know the advantages of living in this community, know the tax future, know what the schools were like. Gather information because what you are trying to do is put together a presentation so that people are going to want to buy this house" -- Pat Burds

Financial worksheet

It is important to have a lender prepare a financial worksheet that shows different scenarios of what the actual dollar cost per month would be to live in your home at a given interest rate and various downpayment amounts. People tend to think about finances on a monthly basis rather than by the year or over 15 or 30 years. The example below shows three different scenarios detailing the expenses involved in paying a mortgage and taxes for three different interest rates and down payment amounts. Information about down payments, closing costs, interest rates and qualifying criteria are all necessary information that will help your buyer determine if they can reasonably expect to qualify for a loan to buy your property

FINANCING OPTIONS
for the Jackson Residence
1234 Greenfield Rd.

Asking price:	$128,900.
Taxes:	$2,200.
Insurance (est)	$90 / month
PMI (5% down)	$80 / month
PMI (10% down)	$50 / month
Loan Term	30 years

	5%	10%	20%
DOWN PAYMENT	$6,445.	$12,890.	$25,780.
LOAN AMOUNT	$122,455.	$116,010.	$103,120.
EST. CLOSING COSTS	$1,094.	$1,083.	$1,060.

		5%	10%	20%
Principal & interest	**9.00%**	$985.	$933.	$830.
Total monthly payment (PITI)		$1,340.	$1,260.	$1,100.
Qualifying income		$57,400.	$54,000.	$47,100.
Maximum monthly debt		$382.	$360.	$310.
Principal & interest	**9.50%**	$1,030	$975.	$867.
Total monthly payment (PITI)		$1,380.	$1,300.	$1,140.
Qualifying income		$59,100.	$55,700.	$48,900.
Maximum monthly debt		$390.	$370.	$330.
Principal & interest	**10.00%**	$1,075.	$1,018.	$905.
Total monthly payment (PITI)		$1,430.	$1,340.	$1,180.
Qualifying income		$61,300.	$57,400.	$50,600.
Maximum monthly debt		$410.	$380.	$340.

ALL FIGURES ARE ESTIMATES
QUALIFYING INCOME & MONTHLY DEBT FIGURES CALCULATED
USING 28% / 36% QUALIFYING RATIOS

Ask a lender you are familiar with to prepare a worksheet like this for you, or most FSBO publishers can probably do it for you. In fact, in many parts of the nation, mortgage lenders are taking an active role in helping the for-sale-by-owner sell the property. The lending business is competitive and lenders are looking to the for-sale-by-owner as a new, relatively untapped market. So call around and see if anyone specializes in helping homeowners like you and see what they can offer. Having a mortgage professional in your corner can be a great comfort, especially when buyers start making offers and you need to be relatively certain they can afford to purchase the property. Your lender will be more than happy to pre-qualify any and all potential buyers you send their way.

Seasonal photo album

Almost everyone has pictures of their home during the different seasons and times of the year. If you live in the snowbelt and you're selling in the winter it's hard enough to imagine what summer is like generally, let alone what your house might look like in the warmer months. Show the buyer how beautiful your lawn is, the flower gardens, the views, a little searching will uncover some really helpful shots.

Pets

Some people are frightened by dogs and some people are severely allergic to animals. Get someone to temporarily take care of your dog and cat. Some buyers may be intimidated by barking dogs, or annoyed by affectionate cats and be turned-off. Don't take chances souring a qualified buyer's interest.

Refreshments

True you're not running a diner, but remember the objective is to make the potential buyer feel comfortable in the home. Consider whether having coffee, tea, soft drinks available would help break the ice, keep a dialog going, or just allow the buyer a little more time to have the thought of living here linger in their mind.

Always remember that these buyers are really interested in your home and are looking to buy. Treat them that way. Below is a brief list of simple tasks to do when preparing for a visit by a buyer.

Checklist of Things to Do Just Before Potential Buyers Visit

• Vacuum carpets, sweep floors & hallways	• Wash dirty dishes
• Display fact sheets and photo album	• Clean up all clutter
• Place fresh flowers on tables	• Pick up clothes
• Scrub sinks, toilets, tubs & showers	• Make the beds

The approach to take when showing your home

Setting the mood of your home

Immediate preparation

Your State of Mind: If you are rushed and hurried, you may impart this mood to the buyer and they may feel uncomfortable in your home. Schedule appointments when you are ready for the buyer. Some buyers will be very eager to see your home and will insist on seeing it now. If you are ready, show it. If not, tell them when they can see it.

Schedule your appointments wisely. Be sure you aren't too rushed before the appointment, or in a hurry to get somewhere later. You need to budget adequate time before and during the visit to devote your undivided attention to the task at hand—selling your home. An adequate amount of time to budget can be from 30 minutes to 1-1/2 hours depending on the size of your home and your pace. One suggestion is to practice showing the home to a friend or spouse, and ask them to critique your performance. This will help you remember key features to highlight, and refine your presentation.

One final consideration is whether or not to have your children around. Only you can determine whether your children's moods, ages and dispositions will be compatible with the calm relaxed mood you've set for your home. If not, arrange for them to be somewhere else during the showing. Give your home the advantage of a calm, cool and confident owner on hand.

"When we showed the house it was just like the cartoon "Family Circus." Jeffy and Barfy were parading along, our kids played with their kids, so the approach we took in showing our home involved the whole family."
-- Pat Burds

The successful buyer visit

Now comes the exciting part! Your home's next owner could be the next visitor through the door. You've done all the major and minor fix-ups needed, you're home looks great! Your home looks great, so you should feel confident and realize that you're in control. You've become an old pro at handling buyer calls and scheduling appointments. Now the first showing is here. It is time for the last important preparation—*prepare yourself!*

Just before the buyer arrives do a final walk-through with a critical eye. Check for clutter, close closet doors, put the toilet seat down. Set out your seasonal photo album, and fact sheets. Put some fresh flowers around to really set the mood.

Now you are ready to focus your attention on creating a welcoming atomsphere in your home—all designed to make the buyer feel "at home."

What do you smell? A guideline to remember is, "If you can smell it, you won't sell it." This goes for pet odors too. No one wants to smell your old dog, or the litterbox, or a full diaper pail. A nice touch might be to have something freshly baked to fill the house with a pleasant aroma, and to serve as refreshments as you chat with the buyers. Reduce odors, produce aromas.

Check the noise level in the house. Is it loud and unsettling? Reduce sources of noise as much as possible. Turn off the dishwasher, washing machine, TV etc. If there is noise outside, try to control it or reduce its impact. Take action to reduce or control the noise, ask a neighbor to mow his lawn after the buyers visit, or shut the windows to block the noise. If you have noisy children, have them visit a friend or relative. Play some suitable quiet background music to set a soothing or relaxing mood.

Like odors and noises, the temperature of your home sends another immediate, although subtle message to your buyers. Either they will feel comfortable or they won't—and that could be because it was too warm or too cold. They may not even be aware of what turned them off, or made they feel uncomfortable about your house! If it is summer, turn on the air-conditioning. In the winter, a cozy fire in a fireplace or woodstove is very soothing. But whatever the season, be sure to have your home at a comfortable temperature.

Lighting can make a huge difference in the mood and appearance of your home. Just before your appointment, turn on all the lights and open the drapes and curtains. A well-lighted room looks bigger and more inviting. Let the buyer see how clean and attractive your home is!

Once the buyers arrive greet them warmly, and ask a question or two to break the ice. Get them to sign your visitor book with their address and phone number so you have a record of who inspected your home. *This is a very important step.*

Don't discount the importance of these seemingly subtle environmental factors in influencing a buyer's decision about the suitability of your home. Some of these factors influence the formation of opinions and our decision making process at complex or unconscious levels. You want to avoid a buyer saying to you, "I don't know why I don't like it, it just doesn't feel right." The steps you take in making your home as inviting as possible will help potential buyers feel at ease in your home, and they'll be more likely to seriously consider living there.

The style to use when showing your home

The objective to be achieved when showing your home is to give the buyers the most favorable impression possible of your home, and adequate opportunity to imagine themselves living there. How best to achieve this goal depends on a number of factors that you must judge "on the spot." At one extreme, you might allow buyers to wander through your home alone so that they have the privacy to freely speak with each other. Allow the buyers to tour your home at their own pace, alone, giving them some general directions as a guideline (e.g. bedrooms upstairs, den downstairs etc.). Make yourself available should any questions arise, but don't shadow the buyers, or be too pushy. After the buyers have gone through the house at their own pace, ask if they noticed specific features of interest. For example, did they notice the new tile in the bathroom? The hardwood floors upstairs were refinished last year, etc. If they missed these features, use it as an opportunity to give a partial guided tour of the house, noting the special features as you go along.

At the end of the unguided tour, you should be sure to mention any special features and offer to take them back for a second look. Here's your chance to point out the best selling features again. Tell your visitors what it is about the house you've always loved, and will miss when you move. Ask them questions to open more avenues to "pitch" your home. If they have children, point out the spacious yard, nearby park, available playmates and high-quality schools. Give the buyers as much information as possible; the longer they inspect the property, the more the idea of living here may grow on them!

The other extreme has you giving a guided tour of each room, pointing out every detail. Perhaps the best advice is to be prepared for both extremes and ask the buyers how they would like to view the home. If you're comfortable giving them free access to your home to view it without you present, offer this option and tell them where they can find you should questions arise. If they choose a guided tour, rehearse your tour with a family member to make sure that you stick to the positive features and don't ramble on, and potentially talk yourself out of a sale.

Whatever approach you take always keep in mind that you've got a highly desirable property and many buyers will want it. Always remember that your attractive home *will sell itself.* Give copies of your fact sheet and financing options sheet to the buyers so they can refresh their memories of your home and what it will cost them.

"I welcome people in and then I tell them to please feel free to browse around, to open closet doors, open anything you want to see. I walk around with them so I can answer any questions they have and I make sure to point out the details. I make sure they focus on what's very special about this house." -- Jeannie St. Pierre.

"We emphasized the biggest selling points first. When people would come up the driveway I would go out and meet them and bring them around to the back deck. The reason was because I wanted them to see the view we have. I would schedule appointments just before sundown so that they would see the beautiful sunset." -- Ben Hale.

What if they don't make an offer or call back?

Sometimes buyers just don't like what they've seen and decide that your home isn't right for them. The most common reasons are:

- ✗ Not in a good location
- ✗ Too expensive, poor terms
- ✗ Size (too big/too small)
- ✗ Poor condition
- ✗ Lacks desired features (large yard, garage, air-conditioning)

On the other hand, some buyers may want to call you, but just haven't done so. They might feel that their calling you would mean they were too interested and they might lose bargaining power. This is nonsense that has nothing to do with buying or selling a home. It's up to you to call them back. Their phone number is in your visitor book. This is why it's crucial to gather this information. Call and ask if they have any more questions, and if they've made any decisions. The call back should occur within 10 days to two weeks after the visit, if you don't hear from the prospective buyers first. Call and identify yourself and state that you're following up. Did they find a home? Do they have any additional questions they would like to ask about your property? Would they like to schedule another visit?

If they have ruled out your property, find out why. Perhaps it just wasn't right for them. Too few bedrooms, too large, etc. However, there could be other reasons that you can do something about. Perhaps you took a risk in not replacing the worn carpeting or not painting the peeling trim. If buyers mention cosmetic reasons such as these for not further considering your place, you should reevaluate your earlier decisions about getting your property in move-in condition.

Another factor that will influence the buyers' decision making process is how long the buyer has been searching for a home in your market. If your home is one of the first that a buyer inspects they may need to get a little more experience in the market before they can appreciate the qualities of your home. As buyers become familiar with the selection that's available their priorities may change. For example, maybe the buyers dismissed your home because it didn't have a fireplace, and they really want a fireplace. Unfortunately, they learn from their experience in the market that homes with the required number of bedrooms and bathrooms in their price range, in move-in condition just don't have fireplaces. The search strategy must change: either the desire for a fireplace must be re-evaluated, or the buyers need to be prepared to spend more. All of this is to say: Call them back, they may be thinking differently about your home as time goes by. Consider most buyers who actually visit your home as potentially interested until they buy something else.

The buyer's point of view

Buying a home is a very important decision. Many complex factors are considered when making that decision. There are practical reasons (number of bedrooms, location), financial reasons (can we afford it?) and emotional reasons. Since you presented the details of your home and price in your advertising, some of the practical and financial facts for these buyers are already known.

Some considerations about the emotional factors that influence home buying decisions. Your buyer is looking for a "home" - not a piece of property measured by square footage alone. A home has a certain, difficult-to-describe feeling that is unique to each owner. Now that you're selling, you may have become emotionally detached from your home and no longer feel the way you once did about it. Try to remember what intrigued you about the house, what special features or characteristics you've enjoyed through the years. Tell the buyer about these...tell them what you're going to miss most about living here. Remember that you are selling a home, not just a house. If the buyers have children, be sure to point out that the park is a block away, or that there are several nice families with children the same age nearby, etc. If the buyers can see themselves as comfortably living in this house, they are more likely to make a serious offer.

How to create demand for your home

Of course, you hope that the first buyers to visit walk in the door, know they found "home" and offer you full price. If you find that buyers appear interested in your home but just don't make offers, you may want to try the following. People arc by nature competitive; nothing is more highly desired than what is also desired by someone else. If someone is interested in your home, letting the cat out of the bag to other buyers can elicit a quick offer. Remember your advantage selling by owner (Exclusive and Special). There is a sense of urgency for a buyer to see your home first, before another buyer does, and if they like it to make an offer. Motivate them to make an offer by tactfully mentioning that other buyers are also very interested. Many will appreciate the call and your concern.

Also, just because a buyer visits your home and does not make an offer doesn't mean they are no longer interested. A buyer's motivation to buy will ebb and flow as other events vary in their lives. Don't hesistate to call up buyers who visited after a couple of days. People are complex. They may really want your home but for some reason they just never get around to calling. You call and ask if any questions came up after their visit, and let them know the house is still available. This is very effective.

"If you have someone who is bringing you a contract on your home, and you have others who are seriously interested, I don't think it's unreasonable to give those other people a call and let them know that this home they had an interest in may be going off the market, and they have an opportunity at this time to act!" -- Pat Burds

So, be ready to field calls and provide information about your home over the phone, plan ahead for visits, set a calm, relaxed mood for yourself and your home and be flexible about how you show your home and the showing phase of the homeselling process will go smoothly and you'll get offers. The next phase of the homeselling process is negotiation.

Chapter 6
Negotiation: The Specific Terms and
Conditions of the Sale

"Trades would not take place unless it were advantageous to the parties concerned. Of course, it is better to strike as good a bargain as possible. The worst outcome is when, by overreaching greed, no bargain is struck, and a trade that could have been advantageous to both parties, does not come off at all." --Benjamin Franklin

An odd situation surrounds the pricing of very expensive items in our society. It seems the more expensive the item, the more negotiable is its price. We would never haggle over the price of a gallon of milk, yet we bargain on cars and homes. Why is this? One reason is general expectations: on expensive things we assume the seller includes "negotiating room" in the price, so buyers reflexively offer less. When selling your own home, knowing your property's appraised value gives you an accurate price from which to negotiate. The appraisal can assure you and the buyer that the price is "in the ballpark" and negotiation can progress from a confident starting point.

When dealing with buyers in a for-sale-by-owner transaction it is important to remember that there is no third party (real estate agent) to act as a buffer between you and the buyer. This arrangement without a middleman is more effective, efficient and leads to fewer misunderstandings because information is not being channeled and interpreted (or misinterpreted) by a third party. Remember two's company, three's a crowd.

People negotiate with each other every day. Spouses, parents, children, friends, relatives and co-workers all negotiate with each other on a regular basis - negotiation is a basic form of human communication. So don't make the negotiation stage of the homeselling process more than it really is -a dialog between a buyer and seller concerning the purchase of a home.

Sometimes buyers may be hesitant to communicate their thoughts and feelings about certain features of your house because if the comment is negative (e.g. I really don't like this color carpet) they will insult or offend you, or if the comment is positive (e.g. I really love this kitchen) you will be more rigid in adhering to your asking price. These games have little or no bearing on the task at hand: selling your home. You, as the seller, should control your emotions. If a buyer says something negative about your home, don't take it personally! Everyone has an opinion and people won't usually point out flaws unless they are considering buying. Remember your objectives; to sell your home within a reasonable period of time, at the best possible price!

One of the most compelling and attractive reasons to sell by owner is that you and your buyer discuss terms face-to-face. Because you meet the prospective buyers, you have a much better idea of how interested they are, what they like about the home, and how serious they are about buying. Most homeowners we have spoken with report that this direct interaction and feedback from buyers is much easier to live with than being in the dark regarding the status of the sale when using agents. When you're out of the loop, letting an agent show the property and interview buyers, you'll wonder how things are going, or worse, wonder why no one has made an offer yet. Taking control of the situation allows you to get instant feedback about the price, condition of the property, terms of the sale etc. This feedback can be useful if you need to modify your selling strategy over time. In fact, many for-sale-by-owner homesellers report that they find some of the buyers "simply delightful," and enjoy the process!

"Our whole negotiation process went extremely smoothly, as there was no middleman to go between the two parties, and actually the people who are buying our house are becoming very good friends of ours" --Ben Hale

Avoiding confrontation

Projecting a relaxed, calm and comfortable mood will reduce the likelihood of a major fear that buyers have when dealing directly with the homeowner: CONFRONTATION. Most people do not actively seek out confrontation, and this is especially so with potential buyers. You must remember that you are temporarily playing the role of a sales person and there are expectations of behavior for people in this role. Be pleasant and congenial, always keeping in mind how much of your equity you're saving selling your own home! In the unlikely event that you encounter a ready, willing and able buyer who is difficult to deal with and challenges every point in the negotiation, remember your bottom line and negotiate accordingly. Try to avoid the situation of winning the battle but losing the war, when the buyer leaves because you didn't compromise on a minor issue. Try to remove as much of your ego from negotiation as possible and adopt a cooperative state of mind with your buyer.

Be consistent with the mood you've set for your home, accurately and fairly price your home, and the negotiations will progress very smoothly. Always remember that since you are selling your own home, you are always 6 or 7% ahead of the neighbor down the street selling through an agent.

Basic elements of negotiation

1. Avoid confrontation. This is not a battle to win. Successful deals occur when both you and your buyer feel you got what you wanted.

Your objective is to sell home for best possible price, while your buyer's is to obtain the home for the best possible price. These are not necessarily competing goals in a for-sale-by-owner transaction.

Buying and selling a home in a by-owner transaction is a WIN/WIN situation for both you and your buyer because you've decided to avoid the real estate commissions.

2. The term or condition under consideration must be negotiable. Know what terms and conditions are subject to negotiation beforehand. Don't be

surprised. Plan ahead! Keep some room to negotiate—remember that the buyer is expecting you to inflate your price. Conceeding somewhat on price makes the buyers feel they got what they wanted, and if the negotiated price is above your bottomline, it should make you feel good too! If you've offered your rock-bottom price, then obviously price is not negotiable. If the buyers must sell their current home before they buy yours, the issue is not negotiable.

3. Willingness to compromise. Being somewhat open to compromise sends a good message to the buyer that you are reasonable, and will do what you can to see the deal completed. Plan ahead of time what is negotiable and what isn't. Do you want to take the washer and dryer, or do you plan on leaving them? Avoid the word "NO" when negotiating. It brings an end to discussion. Remember to cooperate.

4. Trust. It would be nice if you could have absolute trust in your buyers such that when they say they can easily afford your home that it's actually true. Don't rely on trust: rely on objective third parties whose profession is to make good loans, write good contracts, determine fair market value and inspect homes. In the example just mentioned, make the sales contract contingent upon the buyer obtaining a pre-qualification letter of credit from a lending institution within a week or less, so that you're relatively sure they can afford your home.

Preparing to negotiate

1. Foster a calm, relaxed tone.   Be consistent with the relaxed, inviting atmosphere you've created for your home, and there will be less opportunity for distractions and minor annoyances that could derail things.

2. Get everything in writing. Write down what terms and conditions are discussed and agreed upon. Use a worksheet like this one to keep track of what you agree to, and what needs to be worked out. By using the worksheet you can quickly see if you and the buyer agree on the important points and identify which points you must work on. Putting it in writing is a good idea because if you rely on memory it could lead to errors and misun-

derstandings. This worksheet is not to be signed, it simply becomes the framework for the purchase and sales contract that is drawn up and presented to your attorney for review (before you sign it of course.)

Worksheet for Negotiation

Seller's Name...

Buyer's Name/Address/Phone #...................................

Description of the Property(address etc.)

Purchase Price $...

Amount of Deposit, who holds deposit?

          $.......................................Held in escrow

          by...

How long does the seller have to consider the offer?...........................

Financing Considerations

   Pre-qualification letter due (date)..

   When will final loan approval occur?..

   Any seller financing?

Who pays for: points, inspections, appraisals, attorney, repairs?

Personal property included in the sale. e.g. appliances, furnishings, lighting, washer/dryer, etc.

Other conditions of the sale: e.g. Buyers must first sell their current home, Mortgage note not to be at a rate higher than 10%, Property inspection, etc.

Anticipated Closing/Settlement Date.......................................

Rent/day if sellers occupy home after the closing:.................

Note: This document is for preliminary negotiations only and is not legally binding or signed by either the buyer or seller.

What to expect during the negotiation process

Everything and anything in a real estate transaction is negotiable. The first step can be completion of the worksheet where you and the buyer sit down and see how close you are to a deal. Next the buyer should take the worksheet to an attorney and have a formal sales contract drawn up, which they will present to you signed. This step constitutes the OFFER. The contract becomes legally binding when you sign it. If the offer is unacceptable, you could outright reject the offer, or redefine the terms (usually a compromise on an issue) to be acceptable to you—this constitutes the COUNTER-OFFER. Expect several rounds of offer and counteroffer until the deal is acceptable to both of you.

You'll need to agree on the price, amount of deposit, who holds the deposit, date the buyer must get financing, date the buyer takes possession, what other property is included in the sale, and any other special conditions requested by you or the buyer. To protect your interests, have your attorney review any sales contract before you sign it, or include an "attorney approval contingency."

An attorney approval contingency is written into the contract and it allows the buyer and seller to present the contract they have negotiated to their respective attorneys for review. This enables the buyer and the seller to meet with their legal representatives and make sure they understand the ramifications of the contract they are signing. The attorney approval contingency allows each party to renegotiate any other terms to their satisfaction if the attorney advises against entering into the contract. In most cases, the buyer and seller are not likely to renegotiate the price or closing/possession dates. There should be a reasonable time limit specified in the contract for the attorneys to review the contract; 3 to 10 days is common.

Common items and terms subject to negotiation

Here are some of the more common negotiable items that may be part of your sales contract:

Sales price

On the contract, write down the agreed-upon price. Always have the buyer make the initial offer in writing. Avoid the situation where the buyer asks "How low will you go?" and bases the offer on your response. You could be encouraging the buyer to offer less than they were considering offering.

Response time limit

This is how long you have to accept or reject the offer and propose a counteroffer. Usually the timeframe is 48 - 72 hours. Some sellers use an offer from one buyer to leverage activity in other interested but procrastinating buyers. (Some buyers, when they learn that another serious offer has been made, may be motivated to act...possibly with a better offer for you!) For this reason, an experienced buyer may only give you a short time period to consider their offer (e.g. 12 hours, or less).

Deposit

The deposit is money the buyer may offer you as a way to show their commitment to the deal. Most sellers want as large a deposit they can get because they think that if the buyer breaks the contract they get to keep all the money. Not true. You'll probably only be entitled to damages calculated as the direct costs incurred by you because you took your home off the market, probably some advertising money.

A good rule of thumb for the deposit is 1 - 3% of the sales price. The deposit is usually applied to the buyer's downpayment on the property at the closing.

Who holds the deposit money?

The real estate attorney can also perform escrow services. Having a third party hold the money may help the deal along because the buyer will have less worry about getting their deposit back (without suing) should you break the contract.

Financing

The buyer must demonstrate to you that they can get a mortgage for the amount needed to buy your home. Lenders are happy to pre-qualify buyers and send a non-binding letter of pre-qualification to the seller stating that Mr. & Mrs. Jones qualify for such and such amount. This letter is non-binding because it usually relies on self-reported data offered by the buyers. Approval comes later when the lender verifies credit report, income, cash and debt information. A pre-qualification letter due within a week will give you some faith that the buyer does qualify, but remember it's not a guarantee. Ideally, your buyer will be pre-approved for a loan of a certain amount. In effect, the lender has set aside money earmarked for them, and all they need to do is find the right house. This buyer should be highly - valued by you. In essence, pre-approved buyers are cash buyers.

Possession and transfer of title

This is the intended date when you move out and the buyer moves in. Allow enough time to get the loan and find other housing. As a rough estimate, for a conventional loan it takes 4 weeks to get approval and 6 weeks to close—so 6 weeks from signing the contract to moving out. VA/FHA loans takes longer 6 weeks to approve, 8 weeks to close. Ask your attorney what their experience is in your area. Also, unless you put "time is of the essence" in the contract, the deal will not be invalidated by a court for missed deadlines. Mutually agreed-upon time extensions can be added anytime.

Who pays for which items at settlement?

From the signing of the contract to the closing there are going to be expenses that need to be paid. Make sure it is clear what you will be paying for. The following is a list of charges to expect and who typically pays for them—be aware that regional customs may affect who pays for what and, regardless of what is customary, each item is negotiable in any specific contract. Ask your attorney.

> ☛ Loan Origination Fee (points) - buyer
> ☛ Title Search - buyer

☛ Warranty Deed - seller
☛ Hazard Insurance - buyer
☛ Inspections - buyer and/or seller
☛ Appraisals - buyer and/or seller
☛ State/County/City Property Transfer Tax - buyer
☛ Deed Recording Fee- buyer
☛ Property Survey-buyer
☛ Fee for buyer's broker - buyer. As will be discussed in Chapter 9, remember to point out that the lender can include this fee in the buyer's mortgage.

Sale contingent on the buyer selling their current home

Most homeowners probably can't afford to purchase a new home until they sell their current place, or at least have a serious qualified buyer. Here are some points to consider if a buyer gives you a contract with this contingency:

a. Is this ok with you? Do you have other similar buyers without this restriction? Define what you mean by "sell."
b. How long will you give the buyers to sell?
c. Will you keep your home on the market in the meantime, still soliciting offers, giving the current buyer the right of first refusal should another qualified buyer come along? This means that another person may make you an acceptable offer that's not contingent on the sale of their home. The right of first refusal gives your previous buyer an opportunity to remove the contingency (within 48 - 72 hrs), or the contract is void.

The property appraises for the purchase price or more

Many buyers will insist on this contingency because they will probably need to get a mortgage. Remember that chances are you won't get a buyer to overpay for your home, because while a buyer may be foolish, the lender isn't. Anticipating this contingency underscores the importance of accurately pricing your home. If your home doesn't appraise for the purchase price, the buyer is let out of the contract, unless you re-negotiate a lower price.

What personal property is included in the sale?

Most sales include window shades, blinds, screens, shutters, electric fixtures, and light fixtures...these are considered part of the property being sold. Usually, anything that isn't fastened, nailed or attached to the house is not considered included in the sale. For example, is the washer and dryer included with the sale, or are you taking it with you? Portable dishwashers and some woodstoves are not considered part of the house and usually stay with you unless other arrangements are made.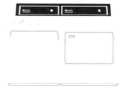

Sale contingent on the house passing inspections?

As we'll discuss in Chapter 8, conveying a structurally and mechanically sound house is not only recommended as a good sales practice, it is also the law in many jurisdictions. In states like California, disclosure by the seller of any know defects in the property is required by law. It makes no sense to hide a defect; sooner or later the buyer will discover it and may sue you for damages. Perhaps the best way to protect yourself is to insist on a home inspection by a competent building inspector. Now the ball is in the buyer's court, if he doesn't opt for the inspection at least you tried. If the home is inspected and undiscovered defects arise later, the inspector may be liable . Get an inspector with errors and omissions insurance. Insisting on an inspection says to the buyer that you have nothing to hide, and some lenders require an inspection before they issue a mortgage anyway. Chapter 8 discusses the home inspection process, and its benefits for the seller and buyer alike.

Consider what happens if the house "fails" the inspection

Is the contract void for any system defect, or only if the repair cost is over a specified amount, and you refuse to make the repair? You probably wouldn't want to let the buyer out of the contract for a minor flaw. Be sure to specify what's minor and major; this can be easily done by attaching a dollar amount to the cost to remedy the flaw. For example, any single repair under $500 will not invalidate the contract. This would define a minor repair as costing less than $500. Repairs to any one system or item over $500 or a combined repair estimate of over $3000 would constitute grounds for contract cancellation on the part of the buyer. This example would define major repairs in terms of both single systems, and aggregate costs.

Rent back provision

What if schedules don't synchronize, with the buyer ready to move in before you're ready to move out? Will you be able to close the deal and rent back from the new owner for a month or two? What will be the rent per day if the sellers continue to occupy after the closing? Be sure to specify the amounts beforehand so there are no surprises down the road. Try not to let a good deal fall through because of a delay of a week or two.

These are some of the more common terms and conditions to be negotiated in a reasonably straightforward sales contract for the purchase of a home. Your attorney will advise you of any special terms to include for your own protection for your special needs and circumstances, if any. Anticipating these "what if" issues is very important, because they do arise often, and it's better to have considered a strategy beforehand than to be caught off guard and make off-the-cuff, rash decisions that you could regret later.

Overview of the negotiation phase

Summarizing the steps for successfully negotiating the sales agreement:

1. Find a buyer.

2. Agree to terms. Use the worksheet to work out the details, and discuss the terms with your buyer in a non-confrontational, cooperative manner.

3. Either with you or alone the buyer takes the worksheet to an attorney, and has a formal Purchase & Sales Contract drawn up. This is much less

expensive than paying an attorney's hourly rate to have them listen to you and the buyer discuss terms and conditions.

4. Both you and the buyer initial the terms and conditions and sign the contract. The buyer backs up their offer with a deposit. Usually the check is made payable to a third party, such as the attorney or an escrow company, or you can hold the check in a separate escrow account.

Chapter 7

The Legal Aspects of Selling Your Own Home

In the minds of many homeowners contemplating selling on their own the most intimidating aspect of a private sale occurs after a ready, willing and able buyer is found. Now what what do I do? The fear that they can't deal with the legal paperwork necessary to sell their own home is a major reason many choose not to even try to sell on their own. Not selling on your own because of the legal paperwork is totally unjustified because whether you sell by owner or with a real estate agent, you will need the professional services of an attorney.

Real estate transactions are legal transactions. Attorneys will be necessary to help you with the contract and to conduct the title search and the closing, so it is in your best interest to consult your attorney as soon as you decide to sell your home privately. Once an acceptable deal is reached between you and the buyer, contact your respective lawyers. The contract will contain information that you and the buyer have agreed to: the date of the closing, loan contingencies, deposits, timeline for financing and other aspects of the sale and purchase. The attorney may also serve as a third party to hold the earnest or deposit money once the deal is struck. Since attorneys are highly involved in the transaction anyway, why not have them help from the start with the Purchase & Sales Contract as well? Knowing the deal is in capable and experienced hands can provide invaluable peace of mind for both you and your buyer.

Choosing a lawyer

Select a good, experienced real estate attorney. If you don't have trusted recommendations, try calling some local banks or mortgage companies for names and recommendations. Sample several sources and start with the names that were commonly recommended. Experienced real estate lawyers will be familiar with the local real estate market and may be able to head off potential problems that could jeopardize the deal. Be sure your attorney knows what you want them to do. Your attorney will perform the following tasks:

- •Draft and review the sales contract
- •Estimate settlement charges to be incurred at closing
- •Hold the deposit money
- •Write the Warranty Deed
- •Help arrange, coordinate and attend the closing

Many lawyers offer "free initial consultations" where it won't cost you anything to interview them and get an estimate for the cost of their services.

What does a lawyer do in a real estate sale?

Draft and review the sales contract

The sales contract is a legal document, so both you and the buyer should enlist the assistance of an attorney to make sure that the proper conditions and terms protecting your mutual interests are clearly stated. Sales contracts can be relatively informal saying that I, Mr. Smith, sell my home to Mr. Jones. If you sign, it's a legally-binding contract. Even though price and the date of the sale are not specified, a court would determine a fair price and enforce the contract. Fortunately, there are good standard contracts available that simply allow you to "fill-in-the-blanks" with the particulars of the sale, such as the price, the date of closing, special contingencies, etc. The contract included here is adequate, with blanks for you to complete with all the appropriate information. You can also pick-up standard contracts at the Chamber-of-Commerce, or legal supply stores for less than $1. A standard Purchase and Sales Contract is included at the end of this chapter.

Conduct a title search (Buyer's attorney)

This process involves an investigative search of town land records over a length of time (usually 40 years) to gather information about the previous disposition of the property. The objective of the title search is to ensure that the person selling the property, is in fact the rightful owner. The attorney will also review any easements on the property. For example, if the town is planning to build a highway in the front yard, a potential buyer would want to know that up front.

If the owner (you) are, in fact, the actual owner, the title is said to be clear and marketable. The attorney certifies the title and usually gives it to a Title Insurance Company. This step protects your buyer from potential claims of long-lost owners if important information was not recorded in the town records for whatever reason. Lenders typically require the buyer to have Title Insurance because if of a long-lost owner makes a future claim, the buyer that the lender gave the money to purchase your home is not the owner so the lender can't re-coup their loan. In such a case, the lender would obtain a settlement from the Title Insurance Company.

Help you meet the terms and conditions of the sales contract

You, working in conjunction with your attorney, should make sure that all the contingencies of the contracts are fulfilled and satisfied. A contingency is a condition that, if not satisfied by a predetermined time, could make the contract null and void, and, in most cases, allow the buyer to get their deposit money back. If an inspection is to be done, schedule it early enough so that if there are any problems you have sufficient time to make the necessary repairs or work out another arrangement with the buyer. Also, many contracts have a final inspection / walkthrough clause in which the buyer has the right to inspect the property immediately before the sale to certify that the home is in proper condition. Most buyers would want a house that is free of your belongings, debris and "broom-clean". Should any problems arise during the walkthrough, the buyer and seller need to negotiate a solution to preserve the deal. For example, if a pile of junk in the backyard was to be removed by the seller but it wasn't, the attorney could add a clause that the seller will put $1,000 into escrow to pay for the clean-up if they fail to take care of the problem by a certain date.

The closing

The closing is also known as settlement or the closing of escrow. Whatever the term in your region, basically what happens at the closing is the buyer gets the title (or legal ownership) to the property and you get your money. Your lawyers, or the title company will probably handle the logistics of the closing which is usually conducted in the office of the lender, title company or attorney. Those present will probably include: you, your lawyer, the buyer, their lawyer, and the lender. You should also notice a significant absence: the real estate agent and the deduction from your equity that would have paid for the sales commission.

Your attorney will have the experience to know what details need to be monitored for a successful closing,but it's helpful that you also know what is required so nothing falls through the cracks. In some areas of the country one person, known as a closing agent, conducts the proceedings at the closing. This can be your attorney, or the buyer's attorney, a representative of the lender, or a representative of the title company. Some title companies and law offices use paralegals, called closers, to conduct the closings their offices are involved in. The closer coordinates the closing with all the involved parties, prepares the closing settlement statements, compares figures with lenders, orders title searches, surveys and other items as needed.

The lender involved may also attend the closing. A buyer obtaining new financing will find that the lender has conditions to be fulfilled to protect its security interest in the property. After all, its really the lender who's buying the property mortgaged to the buyer. For this reason, the lender may require evidence of the following items: title insurance policy; property survey, fire and hazard insurance policy; evidence of proper inspections (termite, structural).

The seller is usually required to show evidence that they own the property by producing a current abstract or title commitment from the title insurance company. If an abstract of title is used, the buyer's attorney will examine it and issue an opinion of title. This opinion states whether the title has any outstanding liens, easements, encumbrances or restrictions that appear in the land records usually stored in the town clerk's office.

When the buyer is obtaining a new mortgage or is paying cash, the seller's existing mortgage is usually paid in full and released. In order to know the exact amount required to pay off your mortgage, you must get a seller pay-off statement from your lender. This will show the unpaid amount of principal, interest due through the date of payment, the fee for the release deed, and credits for pre-paid taxes and insurance.

Sequence of events at the closing

1. The respective attorneys will inspect the title for transfer to the new owner.

2. Your attorney will also prepare a "Warranty Decd" for you to sign. This deed basically consists of a legal description of the property being sold and says that you, the seller, transfer the property to the buyer. It is a legally binding document that transfers the title to the buyer. You sign it and it says that you agree to protect the buyer from losing the property because of outstanding claims against the property. This deed will be recorded by your attorney or the title company at the local courthouse or town clerk's office. You should get a copy sent to you.

You'll need to make sure that you bring certain documents and information with you to the closing. You bring the deed, your mortgage pay-off information, and the most recent property tax assessment. Bring a copy of the sales contract, and bring evidence that any outstanding contingencies have been met. Bring your estimated settlement papers drawn up by your attorney so you know how much to expect from the deal. You may also be required to bring evidence showing the removal of any liens uncovered during the title search, evidence that certain repairs were made, loan documents and property inspection reports.

The buyer needs to bring enough money to cover the costs of purchasing your home, proof of homeowner's insurance, their attorney and the loan officer representing the lending institution. Refer to their Estimated Settlement Statement prepared by their lender. The buyer should also be responsible for scheduling the lender's presence at the closing (double check on this directly by calling the buyer's lender.)

3. The exact closing costs and settlement statements will be prepared and explained to you and the buyer by the attorneys and lender. Your buyer will have received a good faith estimate regarding the amounts they will be required to pay at the closing by their lender. You will receive an estimated settlement statement from your attorney. Pro-rated taxes you owe or are refunded will be determined, the amount the buyers owes will be stated and the amount of cash you get will be determined.

Timeline of events from the signing of the contract until the closing.

Week 1   Negotiations produce sales agreement (contract) drafted
              with help from attorney
              Sales agreement signed by you and buyer
              Buyer applies for mortgage, credit check
              Appraisal scheduled by lender, if necessary

Week 2   Pre-qualification letter received by you from lender
              Title examination started
              Home inspections scheduled, if necessary

Week 3   Title examination completed/problems remedied
              Repairs are started, if necessary.

Week 4, 5 or 6
              Buyer gets mortgage approval
              Buyer does final walk-through inspection
                     (1 day prior to closing)
              Buyer signs mortgage loan documents
              Seller transfers title to buyer
              The deal is completed!

PURCHASE AND SALES CONTRACT

THIS agreement made this....................day of...

Between

       The Seller...of...

          and

       The Buyer..of...

Witnesseth: That the Seller agrees to sell and convey, and the Buyer agrees to buy certain land with the buildings and improvements thereon, located in...

known as or described as... ....

The selling price is...dollars, $.......................................

      Deposit, receipt of which is hereby acknowledged

      and is to be held in escrow account in sum of $.......................................

      Cash or certified check, on date of transfer of title, in sum of $.......................................

DEED: The seller agrees to furnish a duly executed, good and sufficient deed of the property, free and clear of all encumbrances not specifically excepted in this agreement.

POSSESSION: Free of all tenants, personal property, and encumbrances as herein stated is to be given on or before...

      Exceptions:...

TRANSFER OF TITLE: On or before...at..

INSURANCE: The buildings on said premises shall, until the full performance of this agreement, be kept insured against Fire, with extended coverage, in the sum of $ by the seller. In case of loss, all sums recoverable from said insurance shall be paid or assigned, on delivery of deed, to the buyer, unless the premises shall previously have been restored to their former condition by the seller; or, at the option of the buyer, this agreement may be rescinded and the deposit refunded if loss exceeds 20% of the total sale price.

TITLE: If buyer desires an examination of title he shall pay the cost thereof. If upon examination of title it is found that title is unmarketable, this agreement may be rescinded and deposit shall be refunded to buyer, if buyer so elects.

TAXES, water bills, special assessments, rents, and fuel in tanks shall be prorated as of the date of transfer of title.

PROPERTY INCLUDED: All window shades, blinds, screens, shutters, storm sash, electric fixtures, and...

LIQUIDATED DAMAGES: If the buyer shall default in the performance of his obligation under this agreement, the amount of the deposit may, at the option of the seller, become the property of the seller as reasonable liquidated damages.

PRIOR STATEMENTS: All representations, statements, and agreements heretofore made between the parties hereto are merged in this agreement, which alone fully and completely expresses their respective obligations, and this agreement is entered into by each party after opportunity for investigation, neither party relying on any statements or representations not embodied in this agreement, made by the other or on his behalf.

FINANCING: This agreement is contingent upon the buyer obtaining financing in the amount of $...........................

for.................years at the current interest rate, with confirmation no later than... , failing which this agreement is null and void and full deposit is to be refunded to buyer.

BUYER shall present to **SELLER** within ....days, proof of application for financing in the form of a letter of pre-qualification, or pre-approval from a lender. **FAILURE** to provide such proof by said date shall render this contract null and void, at the option of the **SELLER**.

INSPECTION: At **BUYER'S** discretion and expense, an inspection of the property may be ordered. Should structural, mechanical or other defects be discovered, this contract may be terminated by **BUYER** (and deposit refunded) if the aggregate amount of the repairs is greater than $..............., or any individual repair greater than $........... This inspection must be completed by this date.....................

ADDITIONAL PROVISIONS:

....

....

Seller must accept this offer on or before...............................or this offer becomes void.

WITNESS the signatures of the above parties on the day and year written above.

IN the presence of:

x..   ....

      Witness   Date   Buyer   Date

                    ....

                    Seller   Date

Chapter 8

Home Inspections

As mentioned in the previous chapter, the homebuying environment is no longer "buyer beware." When you sell your home, you need to be sure that you have adequately disclosed any problems or deficiencies, both structural and mechanical, to the buyer. You will be responsible for all problems you knew about, or should have known about. In many states, laws are now in place that require sellers to disclose all known, and unknown, defects in the property. If a seller doesn't disclose a problem with the property the buyers can sue for damages, and in some cases win a rescision, which means you buy the property back! By the way, we're not sure how one would go about disclosing an unknown defect either.

In the current homeselling climate, it probably is in your best interest to either have a professional home inspection done prior to putting your home up for sale, or to insist that the buyer have one done. This will help shift some of the disclosure responsibility to a third party professional, the home inspector. However, be aware that some home inspectors will include in their disclosure statements terms to the effect that they are not responsible for anything they didn't find. The best attitude to have about the disclosure process is you want to find any defects in the property and document that the buyer knows about them. This way you can protect yourself from getting an unpleasant surprise later.

There was a recent case in Vermont involving the sale of a home in which the disclosure process became very important. A home was sold in which a known (to the seller) and documented defect was not disclosed to the buyers. The defect involved a faulty natural gas driveway de-icing mechanism: carbon monoxide leaked into the house and killed the family that recently moved in. The defect was previously documented to the seller by a serviceman. The seller was convicted of manslaughter for hiding the defect from the buyers. Ironically, this seller was also a licensed real estate broker.

Guidelines in choosing a home inspector

A home inspector should be experienced and certified by a professional organization. Look for American Society of Home Inspectors, or National Institute of Building Inspectors certification. Some states have licensing requirements as well. Most inspections will cost a couple hundred dollars and take two or three hours. An inspector will probably use a standardized checklist to evaluate each major component of the home. They will produce a written report that will contain their evaluation of the overall condition of the property and any suggested or recommended repairs.

Mechanics of a home inspection

The home inspection process is an orderly sequence of evalutions. The following is a detailed description of the home inspection process, as described by an experienced home inspector. We think that knowing what the inspector is looking for can help you understand the process better, and help you identify potential problems and correct them.

The following is from Mobility Magazine, and describes, step-by-step, the actions and thoughts of a home inspector as he examines a property.

The sight of an inspector around a home inspires different feelings in different people. Sellers experience a sense of nervousness, perhaps, about what the inspector may uncover. Homebuyers usually have hopeful anxiety that no major problems will turn up.

Despite their differences, however, the one feeling all of these individuals have in common is curiosity. Exactly what is the home inspector doing? What is he or she actually looking for with that probing flashlight?

To answer this question, allow me to invite you to come along on a typical home inspection. I would like to share with you some of the observations and thought processes that take place during a home inspection conducted according to the American Society of Home Inspectors' Standards of Practice. With a heightened awareness of what home inspectors look for, you will better understand the home inspection process.

The exterior

Most inspectors begin by taking a long, careful look at the property and the exterior of the home in order to get a general overall impression of the age and condition of the structure. Some of the conditions I find may be clues as to what to look for along the way. When all the pieces of the puzzle are in place, I can develop an idea of the seriousness of a condition.

When an inspector walks around the exterior of a home, it may seem that they are simply wandering from one place to another. However, while walking, the inspector notices many clues about the condition and safety of the property including: sidewalks that have heaved or buckled from tree roots, causing tripping hazards; frayed electric service cables that may allow water to enter the meter socket and start a fire; too few or undersized wires to the home, might mean inadequate service or the potential of overloaded circuits; leaves or debris collecting against the home, which could indicate a water seepage problem in the basement; windows, particularly with southern exposure, that may have paint or glazing problems; windows facing north showing rot or mildew; and earth touching siding or wood, a situation conducive to pest infestation.

One of the most common problems, water in the basement or crawl space, can be apparent even before the inspector sets foot inside the home. Exterior signs of a wet basement include: surrounding ground or a patio that slopes toward the home, possibly directing water inside; missing or broken gutters; disconnected downspouts; and poorly arranged or maintained window wells.

The surest way to identify roof leaks, another common problem, is by examining the underside of the eaves and the roof sheathing during the attic inspection. While outside, however, there are several things I look for anticipate this: missing roof shingles and improper flashing; loss of granules in the joints between roof shingle tabs; cupped, creaked, or bowed composition shingles, indicating advanced age or an overheated attic; and tree branches touching the roof.

The interior

Home inspectors typically conduct their interior inspections methodically; from the bottom up or vice versa, checking each level as they go. I like to start in the attic and pick up clues from the living area as I work my way down to the basement or crawl space.

My examination of the attic allows me to confirm or refute suspicions I may have developed about the integrity of the roof while outdoors. It also provides clues about the adequacy of the home's insulation, ventilation, and exhaust venting. With my flashlight and sometimes a moisture meter, I scan the attic looking for: water stains around the chimney, vent pipes, or other roof penetrations; rust on roofing nails and dark stains on adjacent wood; stains on the attic floor or eroded patches of insulation; excessive discoloration and delamination of decking; sufficient attic openings (screened windows, louvers, or vents) to prevent summer heat build-up and winter condensation; exposed wiring connections and improperly vented plumbing or fan ductwork.

The presence of any of these conditions does not automatically indicate a current problem. They often are signs of a previous problem that has since been corrected. A well-qualified home inspector knows how to tell the difference.

As might be expected, the problems that appear in bathrooms are related almost entirely to water finding its way to where it doesn't belong. Aside from noticing the obvious- water stains or a bucket sitting unceremoniously under a sink-I always check for: evidence of supply pipe leaks, such as greenish pinholes on copper or rust (oxidation) on steel pipes; toilets that "give" when rocked, indicating poor connections and possible water seepage beneath or behind floors and walls; a spongy feeling in the walls around shower faucets and bathtub enclosures, which can indicate a failure of the wall material behind the tile; rust stains on porcelain tubs and sinks, created when water carries with it the debris of deteriorating pipes; and insufficient water flow and pressure, judged by running a number of tub and sink faucets simultaneously.

Although it is impossible to check every square inch of each room and hallway, the inspection of the general living space can produce some very specific indicators about the home's basic heating /cooling and electrical systems. For example: insufficient air flow or dark stains on the wall at the duct register will prompt me to check for dirty furnace filters and improperly sized or disconnected ductwork in the basement; the presence of temporary baseboard or space heaters often is a sign of an inefficient furnace or boiler or distribution system; an abundance of extension cords leads me to suspect an inadequate number of electrical outlets and a possible circuit overload, a serious safety hazard; condensation on the interior of windows can be caused by inadequate ventilation and/or lack of exhaust venting from bathrooms, kitchens and laundry rooms.

Once I have completed my inspection of the living space, I am ready to look around in the basement to confirm the impressions I may have gotten upstairs or outside, and to look for evidence of other problems. While inspecting the basement, I pay particular attention to signs of water or moisture, as well as structural weakness. Some of the conditions I might encounter here include: efflorescence, a whitish mineral deposit, left by receding water or leached through foundation walls; triangular stains in corners, which often indicate water seepage caused by a downspout discharging outside, against the wall; unusual crack patterns or severe bowing or shifting of the foundation; rust stains at the base of support columns; debris collecting at or around the floor drains, which might intefere with their proper function; and sagging floor joists.

Looking more closely at the mechanical equipment located in the basement, I watch for: excessive rust, soot, or cracks at the bottom or lower walls of the heating unit, which often indicate a failed - and dangerous - heat exchanger; puddles of water near a boiler or water heater, perhaps indicating a flawed relief value and/or excessive pressure; a supply of extra fuses beside the fuse box may support my suspicion of an inadequate electrical service and overloaded circuits; and burnt paint or rust on the water heater, which may signal a problem in the burner compartment; a look in the tank flue with a small mirror and flashlight may reveal a distorted baffle.

Sometimes the defects we find on an inspection, rather than indicating a serious problem, simply demonstrate a consistent pattern of deferred maintenance or amateur workmanship. Although they may not necessarily require major repairs, they often indicate the need to generally improve regular maintenance. Samples of these include: open electrical junction boxes and unsecured wiring; dirty furnace filters; "do-it-yourself" store labels on plumbing and electrical components and plumbing or exhaust vents that empty into the attic rather than through the roof to the open air.

When all the evidence is gathered, the next phase of the inspector's job begins: writing the report. The report should provide the client with information about the condition of the property, calling attention to those systems or components that do not function or that need major repair.

In some cases, the cause and remedy of a problem will be identified and specified. In others, the inspector may recommend further evaluation by an expert in the appropriate specialty. Either way, the homebuyer will be better prepared for the transaction, and more satisfied with the purchase. This article was written by Coleman M. Greenburg, a recent past president of the American Society of Home Inspectors, and reprinted with permission from Mobility Magazine.

It's important for you to expect an inspection and prepare for it. Remember that an inspection really protects both you and your buyer. If your home is unsafe, you'd probably want to know about it and fix it. So inspections are not to be feared, but welcomed for the peace of mind they can offer to both you and your buyer.

"Our home inspection was nothing more than to a well-baby visit to the doctors!"--Pat Burds

Also, when you're showing the house to potential buyers you will be pointing out the strengths as well as some of the obvious weaknesses of the property. Consider the following scenario: You tell the buyers that the roof is 20 years old and should probably be replaced, but you haven't done it yet. They decide not to have an inspection, they buy the house, move in and two months later the roof starts to leak badly. They sue you for damages stating that you hid the defect. One way to protect yourself from this happening is to make your disclosures in writing. The form at the end of this chapter is a sample of a Seller's Disclosure Form that you would fill out to the best of your knowledge and present to the buyer. This documents that you have disclosed to the buyer what you know about the condition of the property, which in some cases may be very little. Also advisable is to have the buyer sign an acknowledgement that they actually received your disclosure statement.

Some sellers make the disclosure statement available to anyone who comes through the house; they place it near the fact sheet and financial worksheet. Others prefer to provide such information during the negotiation process. Either way, the disclosure document puts in writing what you know about the condition of the property. However, it doesn't replace the need for a professional home inspection. A home inspection, commissioned by the buyer, is your best means of protection from future problems that the buyer may experience in your previous home.

PROPERTY INFORMATION REPORT

Date:_____

Property address _____   Seller's Name:_____
_____   Buyer's Name:_____
_____

This report provides information about this property. This information is provided by the Seller based on their knowledge of the property. The Seller does not claim to possess any expertise in specific areas that would be relevant to this form (e.g. construction, engineering, architecture, etc), unless otherwise stated. This report is not a warranty of any kind by the Seller. This report is not a substitute for a professional property inspection; which the Buyer can request the Seller agree to as a contingency of a contract for the sale of this property.

Instructions to Seller: 1) Answer ALL questions. 2) Disclose known conditions affecting the property. 3) Attach additional pages if additional information is required. 4) Complete this form yourself. 5) If some items do not apply to this property, write "N/A" (Not applicable). IF YOU DO NOT KNOW THE FACTS, WRITE "UNKNOWN". DO NOT GUESS THE ANSWER TO ANY QUESTION.

A. WATER IN BASEMENT, CRAWL SPACE OR SLAB AREA

Since you have owned the property, has there been any water seepage, leakage, moisture dampness or standing water in the basement, crawl space or through slab areas? __YES __NO. If yes, have repairs been made and, if so what repairs were done and when were they completed?

Are any of the above recurrent problems? __YES __NO. If yes, please explain.

B. MECHANICAL SYSTEMS

Check any of the following items included in the sale which have defects or malfunctions. Do NOT put a checkmark next to ANY item that will NOT be included in the sale of the property.
__Electrical __Plumbing __Sump Pump __Heating __Electronic Air Filter __Hot Water Heater __Heat Pump __Humidifier __Air Conditioning __Well Pump

If any of the above is checked, please explain:

C. APPLIANCES

Check any of the following items included in the sale which are NOT in operating condition or are in NEED of repair or replacement. Do NOT put a checkmark next to ANY item that will NOT be included in the sale of the property. __Range/Oven __Microwave __Hood/Fan __Dishwasher __Refrigerator __Disposal __Washer/Dryer __Trash Compactor __Freezer __Garage Door Opener/ Remote Controls __Indoor or Outdoor Grill __Whirlpool Bath __Hot Tub __Window or in-Wall Air Conditioner __Other:

If any of the above is checked, please explain:

D. OTHER SYSTEMS

Check any of the following systems now on the property that are NOT in operating condition or are in NEED of repair or replacement. Do NOT put a checkmark next to ANY item that will NOT be included in the sale of the property. __T.V. Antenna, Cable Wiring or Satellite Dish __Intercom __Central Vacuum __Security __Fire or Smoke Alarm __Wood Stove __Pool __Attic Fan __Ceiling Fan __Fireplace/Chimney __Exhaust Fans __Other:

If any of the above is checked, please explain:

E. WATER SUPPLY

Property is serviced by (check appropriate boxes): __Public Water Service __Community Water Service __Private Water System __Shared Water System __Well __Well/Pump __Holding Tank __Cistern __Spring __Pond __Spring/Pond/Pump __Water Softener and/or Filters __Unknown Water Pipes are: __Copper __Galvanized __Lead __PVC(Plastic) __Combination __Unknown.

Has Water Potability been tested? __Yes __No. If yes, when?
By whom?   Results:
Has the water supply been tested for Radon Content? __Yes __No. If yes, when?   By whom?
Results:
Are you aware of low water pressure in your water system? __Yes __No.
Has your water supply ever run low? __Yes __No.
If any of the above is checked, please explain:

 Please explain any other problems you have had with your water supply, system or quality:

F. SEWER SYSTEM

Property is serviced by (check appropriate boxes): __Community/Municipal Sewer Available at Street House is connected to: __Community/Municipal Sewer __Storm Sewer __ Septic Tank __Leach Field __Dry Well __Cesspool __Mound System __Other __Unknown.

If other than Community/Municipal Sewer, answer the following: Date Installed:
Date Last Inspected:
Date Last Cleaned: Tank Capacity (In Gallons):   Type of tank: __Concrete __Metal __Fiberglass __Unknown.
To your knowledge, is the system in need of expansion, cleaning, repair or replacement? __Yes __No.
If yes, please explain:

G. ROOF

__Asphalt Shingle __Wood Shingle __Slate __Metal __Tile __Asbestos Composition __Other __Unknown.
 Approximate Age of Roof: Has the roof ever leaked since you have owned the property? __Yes __No.
If yes, has the roof been repaired? __Yes __No.
Do you know of any current problems with the roof? __Yes __No. If yes, please explain:

H. STRUCTURE/COMPONENTS

Check any of the following items which have significant defects or malfunctions: __Foundation __Slab __Chimney __Fireplace __Interior Walls __Ceilings __Floors __Windows __Doors __Storms/Screens __Exterior Walls __Driveway __Sidewalks __Outside Retaining Walls __Other Structures/Components:

If any of the above is checked, please explain:

I. BOUNDARY/PROPERTY LINES

Do you know the location of the boundary lines of the property? __Yes __No
Are the boundary lines of the property marked in any way? __Yes __No __Unknown
Has the property been surveyed? __Yes __No __Unknown. If yes, when? By whom?

J. OTHER MATTERS AFFECTING THE PROPERTY

1. Does the property have Urea-Formaldehyde Foam Insulation? __Yes __No __Unknown
2. Does the property have Asbestos and/or Asbestos Materials in the siding-walls-plaster-flooring-insulation-heating system?__Yes __No __Unknown
3. Has the property been tested for Radon Gas? If yes, when? By whom? Results:
4. Have any of the structures on the property ever had wood boring insects of any type?__Yes __No __Unknown
5. Have there been any wood boring insect and/or pest control treatments done in the last five years?__Yes __No __Unknown
6. Are there any flooding, drainage or grading problems on the property?__Yes __No __Unknown
7. Are there any excessive settling, slippage, sliding or other soil instability problems on the property?__Yes __No __Unknown
8. Is the property located in a Federally Designated Flood Plain?__Yes __No __Unknown
9. Has Seller received written notice of any violations of local, state or federal laws, building codes and/or zoning ordinances affecting the property?__Yes __No __Unknown
10. Are there any easements, shared driveways, party walls, or similar matters that may affect the property?__Yes __No __Unknown
11. Have there been any room additions, structural modifications or other significant alterations or repairs made on the property during Seller's ownership?__Yes __No __Unknown
12. Are there any homeowners association or "common area" expenses or assessments affecting the property?__Yes __No __Unknown
13. Are there any current actions, disputes or lawsuits pending between the homeowners/condominium owners association and any other parties?__Yes __No __Unknown
14. Are there any property tax abatements, land use tax stabilization agreements or other special property tax arrangements applicable to the property?__Yes __No __Unknown
15. Has Seller received notice that the property will be reassessed by any taxing authority during the next 12 months?__Yes __No __Unknown
16. Is the property on a road maintained by the municipality?__Yes __No __Unknown
17. Are there public or private landfills or dumps (compacted or otherwise) on the property or on any abutting property?__Yes __No __Unknown
18. Has there been major damage to the property or any of the structures from fire, wind, floods, earth movements or landslides?__Yes __No __Unknown
19. Are there any underground storage tanks including gasoline, propane and/or fuel oil on the property?__Yes __No __Unknown

20. Have there been any underground storage tanks including gasoline, propane and/or fuel oil on the property?__Yes __No __Unknown

21. Has paint containing lead been used on the property?__Yes __No __Unknown

If the answer to any of the above questions is "Yes", please explain. (Attach additional sheets if necessary):

K. ADDITIONAL INFORMATION CONCERNING THE PROPERTY

1. Approximate age of structures. Main building___. Additional buildings: a)____ b)_____

2. Is Seller currently occupying the property? __Yes __No

3. Is Seller the builder of any of the buildings on the property or any substantial additions, alterations or renovations thereto? __Yes __No If yes, explain:

SELLER'S STATEMENT: Seller provides the information in this report to reduce the danger of DISPUTES or LEGAL ACTION concerning the sale of the property. The information provided herein by Seller does not constitute any warranty, express or implied, about the property. There is no implication that information which is not provided may not be pertinent to a purchaser's decision to buy the property.

Seller acknowledges that the above information is true and correct to the best of Seller's knowledge, information and belief as of the date signed by Seller for those features of the property about which the above information is provided.

Seller_____Date_____

Seller_____Date_____

BUYER/PROSPECTIVE BUYER ACKNOWLEDGES RECEIPT OF A COPY OF THIS REPORT AS OF THE DATE SET FORTH BELOW. BUYER/PROSPECTIVE BUYER UNDERSTAND(S) THAT THIS REPORT PROVIDES INFORMATION ABOUT THE PROPERTY MADE BY THE SELLER(S) AS OF THE ABOVE DATE. IT IS NOT A WARRANTY OF ANY KIND BY SELLER. IT IS NOT A SUBSTITUTION OR REPLACEMENT FOR ANY INSPECTIONS. BUYER/ PROSPECTIVE BUYER MAY OBTAIN A PROFESSIONAL PROPERTY INSPECTION. HOW- EVER, ANY SUCH INSPECTION MUST BE BY PRIOR WRITTEN AGREEMENT WITH SELLER. BUYER/PROSPECTIVE BUYER ALSO UNDERSTANDS THAT THERE MAY BE MATTERS CONCERNING THE PROPERTY WHICH ARE NOT COVERED BY THIS REPORT.

Buyer/Prospective Buyer_____Date_____

Buyer/Prospective Buyer_____Date_____

Chapter 9

Mortgage Basics for Sellers

Offers to purchase your home will probably be contingent on the buyer getting financing. So it is in your best interest to be informed about the types of loans available, the advantages and disadvantages of several types of programs, and determine whether your property is eligible for these types of loans. One piece of advice you could offer your buyer is how to go about choosing a mortgage. Since most of you will also be purchasing another home this legwork can help both you and the buyer understand loan terms and possibly get a better deal.

First of all, we suggest that you shop for a loan, not a lender. Find the best loan in terms of interest rate, fees and points. Also don't assume that "your" lender will "treat you right." The mortgage lending business is very lucrative, hence, very competitive. Mortgage lending is dynamic and innovative, with new, more attractive loan products always becoming available to help lots of different buyers purchase homes,  so check around. Also, consider Mortgage Companies and Mortgage Brokers as sources of loans. Almost 65% of all new loans now originate through mortgage brokers, so consider these as a great resource.

You should be prepared to help your buyers through the loan process. Unless they currently own, they will not know what to do, or even the first step to take. This lack of knowledge is normal, but it could thwart your sale, because if they don't apply for a loan, they won't buy. You may need to help educate your buyer. When you interview mortgage brokers or bankers make mental notes as to who would be the best to have on your "selling team." Who is best able to explain what they do, and how they do it. What steps do they take to ensure that the buyer provides required documents, and how do they ensure that the loan application stays on track. This is important because if you refer your buyer to them, you'll want to be sure that the buyer won't be intimidated by the mortgage loan process and possibly lose interest in buying your home.

We suggest that you actively seek the services and support of a mortgage lending firm that is commited to helping you succeed in selling your own home. Ask if they offer for-sale-by-owner support materials, seminars or consultation. If any mortgage lender tries to steer you away from selling your own home, abandon them and find a helpful company to do business with.

The following is a brief discussion of some of the types of loans available and some of their relative strengths and weaknesses from the point of view of the for-sale-by-owner homeseller.

Conventional loans

Fixed rate

This type of loan locks you into a fixed interest rate for the term of the loan. Your total monthly payment of interest and principal stays the same. These loans usually have 5, 20 or 30 year terms until the loan is paid off. These loans offer predictability: the payment stays the same no matter how interest rates fluctuate. These loans tend to have the fastest turn-around time from application to loan.

Disadvantages of fixed rate loans are that they 1) are usually offered at higher interest rates and 2) require larger down payments. These factors could make it more difficult for certain borrowers to qualify. Also, attractive fixed rate mortgages (those with low interest rates) usually can't be taken over or assumed by another buyer.

Adjustable rate mortgages

Here the interest rate varies across the life of the loan. The amount of variability depends on the movement of interest rates and financial indices (like Treasury bills). As interest rates go up, so will the rate on the loan. Typically, these rate adjustments are made once per year or every three years, and there are strict limits on how much change there can be in a given year and over the life of the loan. Check around; different loans offer different periodic and lifetime caps on interest rates.

A main advantage is the starting interest rates on ARMs can be 1 to 4 percentage points lower than fixed rate loans. This will translate into a lower monthly payment and could help some buyers qualify to buy your home.

Common Requirements for Conventional Loans

*Minimum 5% down   *2 months cash reserves
*Seller can contribute to closing costs
*Private mortgage insurance required with less than 20% down
*Employment qualifications - two year history, typically

Government-backed loans

These loans offer government protection for the lender for a certain percentage of the loan. In other words, if you default on the loan the government will pay back some of the money to the bank, usually around 20% of the loan. Government-backed loans are very attractive because they could help get buyers into homes they couldn't otherwise qualify to get conventional loans for. The major drawbacks are that more paperwork is required and it may take a couple weeks longer to get the loan.

Federal housing authority loans

The Federal Housing Authority (FHA) insures both fixed and variable rate loans. Most downpayments are 5% or less, 3.0-2.5% down is currently very popular. Also, the debt-to-income ratios that are used are more lenient: family housing expenses may not exceed 29% of gross income and total indebtedness may not exceed 41% of gross income.

So a large proportion of income can be used to qualify for an FHA loan. Also, cash-poor buyers can include all closing costs in the mortgage amount; they just borrow more money to pay the points, fees etc. So with as little as 2.5% down a buyer could get into an FHA loan. FHA loans are assumable. If you currently have an FHA loan you may be able to turn over the loan to the buyer on the same terms. The FHA will run a credit check on the buyer to see if they qualify. This could be a great selling point, especially if rates go up! FHA loans also carry no prepayment penalty.

Be aware that as a seller, there are limits on FHA loans. The FHA will not lend on homes over a certain amount (in some areas it's as high as $152,000.) Check what the limits are in your area before suggesting this type of loan to a buyer. Also, the interest rates that lenders attach to FHA loans is not uniform, so have your buyer shop around for the best rate on an FHA loan. Find out now if your home is FHA eligible, it's a great selling feature and will open your home's doors to a greater number of buyers.

Common Requirements for FHA Loans

*Minimum 2.5 - 3% down   *Mortgage insurance required
*Closing costs, can be gift funds *Employment history- 2 years
*Cash reserves - not required

Veteran's Administration mortgage loans

The Veterans Administration (VA) also guarantees loans to eligible veterans. In many cases, no down payment is required. Lenders set the interest rates, so shop around. A drawback to VA loans has recently been eliminated: sellers are no longer required to pay the points on a VA loan, so it shouldn't cost you points to suggest this type of loan. There are limits to how much the VA will insure; currently it's up to $184,000. However, this figure could change so check with a lender.

Common Requirements for VA Loans

*0% down-if qualified   ***Mortgage insurance-none**
*No cash reserves required   ***Can be gift funds**
*2 year employment history
*Closing costs-seller contribution allowed

Direct seller involvement in financing

Besides suggesting suitable loan programs to buyers and opening up new opportunities for them, you can, as seller, also assist in the financing of your buyer's purchase. There are numerous ways to become involved in helping the buyer. Three of the most common forms of seller involvement are briefly described . Whenever considering any type of seller-assisted financing be sure to get guidance from your accountant and attorney.

1. Buy-down the interest rate

Some loans can be had a lower interest rates by paying a fee up-front. This procedure is known as "buying-down" the rate. For example, some programs allow a buy-down of 1% of the mortgage rate for each point paid extra. So paying a $1,000 on a $100,000 loan could buy-down the rate from 9.5% to 8.5%. This will lower the income requirement your buyer will need to meet and could help them qualify. Offering a buy-down should help you adhere more strongly to your asking price because you're helping with financing. So buy-downs could make the difference if you have financially "iffy" buyers. Consult your lawyer about any buy-down arrangement you may be considering.

2. Closing assistance

Some buyers have the down payment but not enough for the various fees (points, taxes, association fees, etc.) associated with getting a loan. You could offer to pay for some of these fees outright. Or you can free-up some of the buyer's money to pay these fees by reducing the final sales price. This is also known as a seller concession.

3. Lease-options to purchase

Here you're trying to find buyers interested in purchasing your property but with little or no down payment money available. These buyers can handle the monthly payments but have no cash to buy at this point in time. The buyer agrees to rent your property for a specific montly rental amount and to pay for the right to purchase the property at an agreed-upon price within a fixed time period. The option fee which can include both a one-time fee of 3 - 5% of the purchase price and a fixed monthly fee, are both credited toward the purchase price. One way to think of a lease-option is as a forced down payment savings plan for your future buyer. The buyer eventually saves enough to purchase, and you get a good price. If the potential buyer chooses not to exercise the option to buy, the option fees are yours to keep. This motivates the renter to buy. Consult your lawyer about the tax consequences of becoming a landlord, and the details of the arrangement.

Pre-qualifying your buyer

One of the important questions that concerns you is, "Can these people afford to purchase my property?" The best way to find out is to have them see a lender and apply for a loan. The lender will take income, debt and credit history information and determine whether they "pre-qualify". The lender will send you or your attorney a pre-qualification letter stating that your buyers qualify or don't. Do not hesitate to ask lenders to perform this service for you! This is how they get their loan business, and they will welcome anyone you send to them with open arms.

Sending the buyers directly to a lender is smart because it prevents the uncomfortable situation of you asking for financial information about your buyer. While it is certainly reasonable for you to ask the buyer, "How much do you make?" , it can be awkward. Consider the following. Buyers are interested in the details of your property. Would you be offended if they asked you when was the kitchen last painted or the septic tank last pumped? Of course not, these are reasonable questions in this context. Likewise, your biggest concern is the buyers financial capability to purchase your property. Be diplomatic. Asking questions like "Is this in your price range?" and the justification for their response will tell you whether they've got a clue as to whether they can afford it, been to a lender, or are simply dreamers.

The best way to handle questions about the buyers finances is send them to a lender for pre-qualification, and have the lender send to you a letter within 3-7 days stating that these people would probably qualify or not. "Probably?" Pre-qualification letters are issued by lenders as a pre-liminary move. The data are self-reported by the buyer and not verified by other means, other than a credit report. So until employment and bank deposits are verified, and debt ratios are determined, qualification is not definite.

Some buyers will come to you saying they have been pre-qualified for a certain amount by a real estate agent. The wide variety of programs available and the complexity of the process has virtually eliminated the ability of a traditional real estate agent to perfom this service. Suggest that your buyer contact a mortgage company-perhaps the company that prepared your financial worksheets -for a pre-qualification meeting. This move on your part will increase the chances of getting a qualified buyer and actually selling your property.

In fact, many buyers are becoming savvy about home purchase issues and arrange for a pre-qualification letter to be produced so that they can shop with this document in hand. Also, some mortgage companies are now issuing "credit" cards to buyers which state that they have been approved for a mortgage of a specific amount. Often these credit cards will have the phone number of the mortgage company on it so you can verify the information. Obviously, buyers pre-approved for a mortgage amount that covers your asking price are to be considered "hot prospects" by you, at least you have less worry about their financial capability.

If you can't wait these few days for a letter from a lender you could also get a rough idea by calculating the monthly mortgage payment for your property based on your sales price at current interest rates with 5, 10 or 20% down. Ask a lender to prepare this financial worksheet for you. Most for-sale-by-owner publishers can generate this for you as well. You should have this present, along with your fact sheet, when buyers come to inspect your home. Next, have the buyers determine whether they can afford that amount by "qualifying themselves." Clues that you can look for are: stable employment records, approximate aggregate income, and the value of their present home. Remember that lenders may use different formulas and ratios to determine the maximum amount of a loan and the creditworthiness of borrowers.

Mortgage loan pre-qualification chart

Most lending institutions use similar methods to calculate the amount of a mortgage that a borrower can reasonably afford. The steps below will allow you to determine the approximate price-range that is appropriate.

The following calculations are similar to those that lenders will use to qualify borrowers for a conventional mortgage (a conventional mortgage loan means that there is no government insurance backing the loan). Government-insured loans like Veterans Administration (VA) and Federal Home Administration (FHA) may have more lenient requirements.

1. Monthly Gross Income (before taxes) = A
2. How much you can afford to pay for monthly housing
   expenses (includes mortgage, taxes & insurance) Multiply A by .28 = B
3. How much can you afford for a monthly mortgage payment
   (Principal & Interest) Multiply B by .80 = C
4. To determine a mortgage amount: Select an interest rate from the Mortgage Chart and divide C by the interest rate factor. C / interest rate factor = D. Multiply the result D by 1,000. = E.

This is the dollar amount of the mortgage you can afford.

5. Factor in how much you want to place as a down-payment, and how that will affect how much you can afford. All else being equal, the larger the down-payment , the more "house" you can afford.

Down-Payment (%)	Divide By (F)
5%	.95
10%	.90
15%	.85
20%	.80

E / F = Approximate Price of the House You Can Afford

One final consideration: if you have substantial fixed monthly payments for credit card expenses, car payments etc, these obligations will reduce your gross monthly income and the mortgage amount for which you will be eligible.

Mortgage Chart

Interest Rate	Factor for 30 yr	Factor for 15 yr Mortgage
7.0	6.65	8.99
7.5	6.99	9.27
8.0	7.34	9.56
8.5	7.69	9.85
9.0	8.05	10.15
9.5	8.41	10.45
10.0	8.78	10.75

Sample Worksheet

1. Yearly Income = $40,000 / 12 = $3,333 (A)
2. $3333 x .28 = $933 (B)
3. $933 x .80 = $746 (C)
4. Selected a 7.0%, 30-yr mortgage—factor is 6.65
   $746 / 6.65 = 112.18 (D)
   112.18 x 1000 = $112,180 (E)
5. With a 5% downpayment
   $112,180 / .95 = $118,084

$118,000 is the approximate price of the home that can be bought.

How Much are the Monthly Payments? Monthly payments for a 30-yr loan at various interest rates

Amount of Loan	6.5%	7.0%	7.5%	8.0%	8.5%	9.0%
$70,000	$442.45	$465.71	$489.45	$513.64	$538.24	$563.24
$80,000	505.65	532.24	559.37	587.01	615.13	643.70
$90,000	568.86	598.77	629.29	660.39	692.02	724.16
100,000	632.07	665.30	699.21	733.76	768.91	804.62
110,000	695.27	731.83	769.14	807.14	845.80	885.08
120,000	758.48	798.36	839.06	880.52	922.70	965.55
130,000	821.69	864.89	908.98	953.89	999.59	1046.01
140,000	884.90	931.42	978.90	1027.27	1076.48	1126.47
150,000	948.10	997.95	1048.82	1100.65	1153.37	1206.93
160,000	1011.13	1064.48	1118.74	1174.02	1230.26	1287.40
170,000	1074.52	1131.01	1188.66	1247.40	1307.15	1367.86
180,000	1137.72	1197.52	1258.59	1320.78	1384.04	1448.32

Timetable of the mortgage process: From application to closing

Week 1 • Purchase & Sales Agreement Signed

• Buyer applies for mortgage

• Escrow is opened and earnest money deposit placed

Week 2 • Preliminary qualification letter sent by lender

• Necessary inspections are ordered

Week 3 • Title search is completed

• Termite work and other repairs are performed

Week 4 • Title problems (if any) are cleared

• Lender approves loan to buyer

Week 5 • Buyer does final walk-through of property

Week 6 • Buyer signs loan documents

• Seller signs off on title

• Deal is closed

Chapter 10

Dealing with Real Estate Agents

When selling your own home, you will be approached via telephone, or in person, by real estate agents trying to get you to list your property with them. Some will send letters touting their expertise in selling; others will call you saying they have just located an out-of-town buyer for you and others will show up at your door. You, the private homeseller, are a major concern of the real estate industry. If you sell without an agent, it will encourage others to sell without agent; eventually there will be little need for listing agents.

In an attempt to preserve their business a major thrust of the real estate industry's marketing campaign is to discourage and thwart your attempt to sell on your own by contacting you by mail, telephone or in person. This is primarily accomplished by presenting the homeselling process as very complex and time-consuming -- assuming that you are uninformed.

Some real estate agents use tools like these videotapes to confuse you and get you to list your property with them. For example, when you advertise your home for sale by owner in the local newspaper, not only do buyers see the ad but so do real estate agents. Real estate agents will either call you up or drop by with this "helpful" videotape called *Selling By Owner*.

The brochure that markets the video to agents describes the tape as *"a friendly counselor approach that shows FSBOs how time-consuming and complex a real estate transaction is...and why it should be in professional hands. A great prospecting tool to overcome FSBO objections...and it gets them to list with you!"* Interesting isn't it! For this type of mis-information the producer of the video received the National Association of Realtors Outstanding Educator Award.

This System Turns FSBOs Into Listings!

Agents will give many reasons why you shouldn't try to sell your own home. They may point out that you could set the wrong price, accept unqualified buyers or, waste your time. All of these things could happen to naive sellers - but they can occur even if you list with an agent. The best way to prevent mistakes, when selling on your own, is to understand the home selling process from start to finish, which you have accomplished.

Types of real estate agency listing contracts

There are also some rare instances where an agent can be useful to you and the buyer pays their fee. So it's important to understand the different types of listing arrangements and what they mean for you, the for-sale-by-owner seller. And remember: Usually the person or company presenting you with a contract to sign is protecting their interests at the expense of yours. Rule #1 is: DO NOT sign any listing agreement unless you thoroughly understand what you are signing away. If in doubt, have your attorney explain the contract to you BEFORE you sign it.

Exclusive right to sell

This will be the first type of listing offered by the agent. The agency you sign this contract with will be entitled to the sales commission no matter who sells the home or how it is sold. If you sell it through your own advertising, or if a neighbor buys it, you still owe a commission. If the agency sells it, they get a commission. Obviously, agents like this type of listing, and may present it to the naive homeseller as the only option. Keep in mind that when you sign such an agreement often you have effectively lost the right to change your mind about selling. If a full price offer is presented to the agency and you refuse the offer, you are obligated to pay the sales commission. This lack of freedom of choice is a major drawback to dealing with agents.

The exclusive-right-to-sell contract is really a sucker's contract. It protects the real estate agency at the homeowner's expense. Essentially, your hands are tied. If you feel that the agents aren't doing enough to sell it, you're trapped for 3, 6, or 12 months because you signed a contract.

Exclusive agency

A commission is paid only if the agency you signed the contract with brings the buyer. In effect, you retain the right the sell it yourself, and are in competition with the agency for the sale; at stake is the commission. Some owners going this route will retain their competitive advantage by listing the house at a higher price with the agent (to cover the cost of the commission) and offering a lower price to buyers who come directly to them. Clearly the buyer will be paying the commission when going through a real estate agent.

Also, retain your lists of buyers who visited your home or called in response to your ad, people who contacted you first should not be counted as agent-acquired prospects. Be sure to clearly specify this in any listing contract. With this type of listing, it is important for you to remember that you have legally retained the right to sell your own property, and in effect are competing with the real estate agency that has listed your property. Whoever brings the buyer gets the commission. If a realtor brings a buyer, you will pay 6 - 7% or more. If you find your own buyer, you will pay nothing.

When you get your buyer, the first thing you should do is call your real estate agency and get their complete list of buyers who saw the property through them. Do not tell them who your buyer is. Get their list as soon as possible, within hours, if possible. Have them sign a statement to the effect that this is the complete list so that "phantom" buyers can't occur. This will prevent your buyer from suddenly appearing on the agent's list. It happens.

Open listings

Open listings are also known as non-exclusive listings. This means that the property is open to anyone who has a buyer. The agent who brings the buyer gets a commission; however, you still retain the right to sell and you probably are still doing most, if not all, of the advertising and marketing of your home. This type of listing is usually considered by some sellers in tough markets to gain access to a new pool of potential buyers- those that are working with real estate agents. Agents who are working with buyers trying to help them find a home are not likely to suggest a buyer see your home if they don't stand to benefit from the transaction. An open listing says that you are willing to pay a reduced commission (1, 2, 3, 4%) to an agent bringing you a buyer. Obviously since you've probably invested in the expense of marketing your home and the agent hasn't, it would be ridiculous for you to pay a full 6-7% commission. Functionally, this type of listing can help you because it may get agents to consider suggesting your home to their clients if the client's don't see it on their own. However, if you effectively advertise your home, chances are a conscientious buyer scouring the publications will see your ad and call you, and both of you can save.

The final word on this type of listing agreement: You retain the right to sell on your own. Listing agents don't like this type of listing because they won't get a commission unless they personally bring the buyer to you. They probably won't go to much effort to market your property, since someone else (including you) is likely to reap the benefits of their efforts. Usually you pay a reduced commission in an open listing agreement. You must negotiate the amount of the reduced commission. The contract should only pertain to the particular buyer - by name - that the agent has brought. If that buyer doesn't purchase, you owe the agent nothing.

Flat fee arrangements

The agent agrees to work with you as a consultant, and assist you with the marketing, negotiation and/or paperwork on a fee-for-services basis. For example, the real estate agency might split the cost of advertising with you in exchange for your agreeing to show the property and negotiate with prospective buyers. Or they might ask for 1% to "handle the paperwork and closing details." Everything is negotiable. Depending on your specific situation, this type of arrangement may be of use to you.

As a FSBO homeseller, if an agent approaches you with an interested buyer, and you are truly interested in their buyer, your best bet may be to offer them an open listing for that buyer only. Be sure you specify how much commission you agree to pay if this buyer purchases the house! The agent will probably ask for 6% -- don't agree to more than 1 - 3%, if this fits your game plan! Remember - you've done all the work, the agent and buyer know your home is for sale because of your effective advertising efforts.

One tactic to consider is refusing to negotiate any fee, and let the buyer decide whether they wish to continue their allegiance with this agent or go it alone. We've heard many reports of buyers who return to for-sale-by-owner properties they see while "caravanning" with agents...and eventually purchasing the property! Remember, property offered for-sale-by-owner is more attractive to buyers because they know they stand to get a better deal.

Discount real estate services

Another option that may be available to you is a more reasonably priced "discount real estate service." Instead of the typical 6 -10% commission rates, discount real estate companies reduce their charge in exchange for your participation in selling the property. These companies may charge anywhere from 2 - 4%. You may be required to show the property (your strength) and pay for some or all of the advertising costs. Discount programs offer pre-sale counseling and advice on pricing and preparation as well as help negotiating the deal. Depending on your situation this lower cost option may be something to look into. The major benefits of these programs still rely on the strengths and benefits of for-sale-by-owner real estate.

Temporary listing contracts

An agent may call you or show up at your door with a bona fide buyer. One way to handle this situation is to construct a short-term custom agreement between you, this agent and this buyer. The temporary listing agreement should state the agents name, your name and the buyer's name, the amount of the commission (if any), and the selling price of the home. Some sellers temporarily inflate the price to compensate for this commission. The commission should be less than full because you have paid for the advertising. This is a very personalized and specific agreement and should be valid only for a short period of time (1 - 2 days).

It's advisable to call your lawyer for on-the-spot advice if you're uncomfortable with anything in the contract. Slow down and be patient; don't be hurried by an agent with an agenda. If that buyer is truly interested, they will wait. Don't allow yourself to be pressured into a snap decision that you'll regret later.

Buyer brokers

A relatively recent development in the real estate industry is the relationship in which an agent helps the buyer find a suitable property with the buyer paying their fee. This means that the real estate agent represents the buyer, and probably will negotiate on behalf of the buyer.

Buyer brokers evolved, in part, because usually the broker works for the seller to get the best deal possible from the buyer. Buyers objecting to working with someone who does not have their best interests in mind demanded an arrangement where the broker works for them - the buyer broker. Here the tables are turned with the buyer paying a commission or fee to the broker for their services in locating and negotiating the best price.

Although the buyer is technically responsible for the agent's fee, they, the buyers and/or the agent, usually request that this be negotiated as part of the seller's closing costs. So the broker may ask you to agree to a 3% commission before showing the property to their buyer. Often, the fee is built-in to the buyer's mortgage in the form of a higher selling price. For example, if the sales price of the property is $100,000, a sales price of $103,000 may be offered to you with the understanding that the "extra" $3,000 be rebated to the buyer. The buyer would, in turn, pay the buyer broker the $3,000 fee.

A good tactic to use when approached by a buyer broker is to avoid making any concrete arrangements upfront until you've received an offer from the buyer. Rather, tell the broker that you are open to paying a portion of their fee, but want to wait until you see the amount of the offer. Don't sign any contracts to list your home (contracts like those described above) that buyer's brokers may present to you. The best contract a buyer broker should present to you is a signed purchase offer from a buyer who is, hopefully, paying the agent's fee as well.

Consider the likelihood of being approached by a buyer broker, to anticipate the situation and how this may affect your asking price. If buyer's brokers are plentiful in your area it is wise to factor the possibility of your paying a partial commission into your asking price.

Also, BEWARE!!- In some parts of the nation, a buyer broker can legally negotiate a fee from both you AND their buyer!! This is called dual agency. While we would hope not many would do this, we've heard stories from customers about this happening. Ask the buyer broker point blank what their payment arrangement is with their buyer, or speak directly with the buyer yourself. Be sure s/he isn't taking 3% (or more) from both of you!

Bad buyer brokers

One final thought on buyer brokers. Only true, exclusive buyer brokers are useful to for-sale-by-owner homesellers. Unfortunately, many listing agents masquerade as buyer brokers, wolves in sheep's clothing if you will. Consider the following scenario: an agent will draw in a buyer looking for a certain type of home, and the agent will seduce the buyer with the idea that it won't cost them anything for the agent's services, "we'll get the seller to pay for that" is the usual line. The agent, having burned the bridge of receiving a commission from the buyer, now must get a fee from you, the for-sale-by-owner seller. Next, the agent will approach you with the enticement of having the ideal buyer for you place, and they'd love to show your home to this buyer but first you must list it with their agency for a short period of time - perhaps 6 months! If you agree, you'll owe a full commission fee if there is a buyer, or be stuck in a listing contract if that buyer doesn't materialize-which mysteriously happens very often in these circumstances. Often, the mythical out-of-town, perfect-for-your-place, pre-approved buyer dangled before you, along with the listing contract, will suddenly vaporize once you sign on the dotted line. Which probably means there never was any buyer. The agent was just operating as a listing agent using the trick of buyer brokering to fool you into listing the property with them. Remember the objective of the real estate game: list it and forget it. Buyer brokers of use to you *do not list property*.

Good buyer brokers

True buyers brokers don't list any property; they only work with buyers who are responsible for paying their fee. Exclusive buyer brokers such as these will show for-sale-by-owner properties without hesitation be-cause they know they're better deals compared to agent - listed properties. The most effective way to determine whether you're dealing with a true buyer broker is to ask if they list property: if they do forget them!

National companies that are exclusively buyer broker is Buyer's Re-source or The Buyer's Agent. If you feel comfortable negotiating with a buyer who has professional representation, taking the initiative and sending the local exclusive buyer agency your fact sheet would open up this avenue for you.

Questions about real estate agents

The following questions are from private homesellers regarding their experiences with real estate agents. The purpose of this section is to present some of the possible scenarios you may encounter so that you can quickly recognize them and effectively deal with the situation.

Won't agents steer buyers they are working with away from private sales if there is no commission involved for them?

Yes, they most likely will. Why should an agent tell a buyer about your home ($0 commission) when they can show homes that the buyer may purchase with a commission? To appeal to buyers currently working with agents in a non-contractual manner, you must, in your advertising, convey that your home is a better buy compared to a comparable home listed with an agent. Also, true buyer brokers (those without an agenda of listed homes to sell) are eager to advise their clients about your private sale home because quicker sales can be made.

Real estate agents, with all their resources and experience, must sell all or most of the property that is assigned to them. Do you have any information on this?

Properties listed with real estate agents are at a competitive disadvantage compared to other property on the market. In fact, up to 60% of all real estate agency listings expire. That means that after 3, 6 or 12 months of trying to sell with an agent either the owner gives up to tries to sell it on their own.

Interestingly enough, there is such a large number of expired listings that some real estate educational material teaches agents how to acquire other agents' expired listings. The videotape producer we mentioned before, the National Association of Realtors Outstanding Educator, has a specialized video called "Expired Listings" Here's what the blurb, designed to be read by real estate agents, says, *"30-60% of all listings expire...a great source of potential business! This explanatory video covers the three main reasons for expiration: Marketing, Condition and Price. Sellers learn how to analyze and improve each of these areas using your services. 'Expired Listings' encourages them to list again...with you!"*

So the real estate industry acknowledges its failures and devises a scheme to keep naive homesellers in the loop. Basically, they place the blame for the home not selling on the bad service of "another agent" or the seller (price too high, poor condition of home). We have even noticed agents advertising themselves as specialists in handling expired listings. It's clear that if you want to sell your home fast and net the maximum amount of equity, you need to do it right the first time...sell it yourself!

One benefit that agents have is the multi-list service. Won't I be missing out on this exposure if I sell on my own?

First of all, it's debatable whether the multi-list service is a benefit to the seller. As discussed above up to 60% of all listings with real estate agents expire, so it can't be that effective in selling homes after 3, 6, or 12 months. Also, it is important for you to understand the purpose of the multi-list from the agent's point of view. The goal of the real estate broker is to get listings. The more listings they get the more potential money they can make because the listing agency always receives one-half the commission, with the selling agency getting the other half. If the listing agency also brings the buyer, they get the entire commission. So agencies are motivated to try to sell their "own" listings first, for the entire commission.

Agents also use other homes in the multi-list as comparables. For example, one ploy is to find a similar home listed by another agency at a higher price or lacks some cosmetic appeal. They show the buyer the less desirable home first, then they show their listing next. The buyer is fooled into thinking they are making a shrewd decision in selecting the second home unaware that they have only been show a carefully selected sample of those available. And of course, they haven't been shown any for-sale-by-owner properties.

When I was selling my own home I got a lot of calls from real estate agents trying to convince me to list with them. Some were polite, they made their sales pitch and that was it, however, others were persistent and annoying. Is there anything I can do to avoid this?

Remember, the real estate industry will never help you sell your own home, so be wary of any agent offering to "help." Unfortunately, the private homeowner who exercises their right to sell their own property is a major source of business for real estate agents. They call it "prospecting." Agents realize that many homeowners have unrealistic expectations about how long it will take to sell a home; why do you think they sign you up to 3, 6, or 12 month contracts? Uninformed homesellers are vulnerable to agent's demoralizing tactics and rhetoric. Of course, agent's have a surprise in store when they contact you - an informed, motivated homeseller. Agents will offer free market analyses, and "helpful" videos in an attempt to get a foot-in-your-door. All of these tactics are designed to discourage you from selling by owner, and to list with that agent.

Just because you've chosen to sell your own home doesn't give real estate agents the right to harass you, and invade your privacy and the sanctity of your private residence. If an agent calls and you don't want them to call again, simply tell them that your phone number is for buyers only and that they're not to call again. A federal law has been enacted to help you deal with persistant problems. The 1991 Communications Act protects consumers from unwanted, unsolicited telephone calls for the purposes of selling goods or services. The standard fines for violation of this law range from $500 to $1500 per offense. You're the consumer, and the real estate agent is the telemarketer. Consider the following insight: only ineffective agents will call on for-sale-by-owner properties.

In 1997, for the ninth consecutive year Gallup Research found that real estate agents were among the lowest rated occupations with respect to integrity and honesty. Only car salesmen and lawyers rated lower than real estate agents when people were asked to rate the honesty and ethical standards of people in a variety of fields. FYI: pharmacists, clergy, medical doctors, college teachers and dentists rated the highest.

THE WALL STREET JOURNAL.

Teacher gives real estate agents below-average grades on ethics

by Mitchell Pacelle, Staff Reporter for the Wall Street Journal

©The Wall Street Journal, Dow Jones Inc.

Are real estate agents getting a bum rap?

Deborah Long, a Boca Raton, Fla., real estate agent and educator, thought that might be the case. After all, the American public consistently gives the profession low grades on ethics. In a 1993 Gallup Poll that ranked 26 professions for honesty and ethical standards, real estate agents placed a dismal 19th--below even lawyers and television talk-show hosts.

So as part of her fieldwork for a doctorate in education, Ms. Long administered a test that measures ethical reasoning to dozens of real estate agents who attended classes at a vocational school where she teaches.

It turns out the American public was right. "It appears that real estate people are ethically immature," she says.

The 82 Florida agents who took the Defining Issues Test, a standardized test developed by the University of Minnesota, averaged a score of 35, compared with a score of 40 for typical adults. The agents ranked just above high school students in their ability to make ethical judgements.

Ms. Long also found that agents earning $30,000. to $40,000. demonstrated a lower level of ethical reasoning than those making $10,000. to $20,000. Agents with more than 10 years of experience scored lower than less experienced ones, she says.

Ms. Long cautions that her test measured only ethical reasoning, not ethical behavior. But these appears to be cause for concern about behavior, as well. In 1993, the public filed 5,400 complaints against Florida agents, the highest ratio of complaints to active agents in six states Ms. Long analyzed.

St. Louis broker Bruce Aydt, vice chairman of the professional standards committee of the National Association of Realtors, questions whether Ms. Long surveyed enough agents to produce valid results. Jerry Matthews, executive vice president of the Florida Association of Realtors, adds that most ethical problems involve agents that don't do much business.

Ms. Long even offered a 15-hour intervention program to some of those she tested in an attempt to raise their ethical skills. At best, real estate agents were able to elevate their scores only to the level of adults in general. "But that doesn't mean they're going to behave any differently in the field," she adds.

The media and for-sale-by-owner real estate

Recently the *Boston Globe* ran a well-researched story on the process of selling your own home. The article was well received by the general readership and by homeowners, in particular. However, the following week, there was a flood of letters to the editor by real estate agents complaining about the story. The following letter epitomizes a general attitude of some agents toward the media, and importantly illustrates the message embodied in the previous *Wall Street Journal* article.

Article on FSBOs was slap in face to real estate companies and agents.

On behalf of the dedicated and hard working agents in this office, I feel compelled to respond to your recently published article regarding owners selling their own home. The article, written by Mary Sit, is a slap in the face to the real estate companies, including this firm, who pay your writer's salary, and yours, through advertising revenue.

Real estate agents, like everyone else, are working to earn a living. We rely upon our knowledge and expertise to bring two parties together in an arms-length transaction, and for that service we charge a fee. Since FSBOs contribute some revenue to your paper you may feel justified publishing an article on their behalf. Common sense should dictate that the article would be sized relative to revenue produced. FSBO ads for the most part are quite small. Your paper would benefit by producing articles which promote the services of professionals. This would not only increase our listing base, but it would increase the size of advertising, thereby increasing revenues to the Globe.

Several years ago the Greater Boston Real Estate Board considered publishing its own real estate newspaper. Perhaps now that the recession has ended it is time to reevaluate this idea, as you have made it extremely clear that our money will be better spent elsewhere. In the meantime, I urge you and your staff to consider writing articles promoting the industry that pays you

.John McCormick, General Manager, The Prudential West Realtors November 7, 1994.

The attitude expressed in this letter clearly is that the media should not help the homeowner, rather, its role should be to help the real estate community get more commissions from the homeowner. Furthermore, to suggest that only pro-realtor articles be written because they pay for advertising in newspapers is small-minded. My guess is that this letter was not intended by the writer to be published, but rather intended as a private threat to the editor.

We are by no means experts in the workings of the media but we have noticed some very disturbing events with regard to newspapers and real estate, which suggest that the above threats may be more common than we realize. We suspect that many newspaper and magazine editors fear the backlash from local real estate agents if they were to print a story about a product that helps homeowners sell their own homes. We have also noticed that many syndicated real estate columnists are also "in the real estate community's pocket" in terms of the stories they choose to cover, and in particular how they treat the for-sale-by-owner movement. The practical and financial advantages of selling your own home appear clear to everyone, except the majority of these writers. True most have a slanted perspective, because they are, or have been, real estate agents, but they should at least acknowledge that selling your own home makes the most practical and financial sense to the homeowner. (Of course, my bias is showing through as well).

Chapter 11

How to Sell Your Own Home: Summary and Review

This section covers many of the highlights of the previous chapters. It is intended to serve as a quick reference and to serve as a memory refresher. Consult the topic of interest and the information presented here should trigger a flood of memories from your previous readings of the entire chapter devoted to that subject.

1. Make the commitment to sell on your own.

Develop realistic expectations: Many homesellers think that they will sell as soon as they put a sign in the yard. This is very unrealistic. In some markets, it may take 3, 6, or 9 months or longer to sell some homes. Find out what the average time on the market is for a house like yours and be prepared for it to take that long. A good source for this information is your local newspaper, town clerk's office or real estate board. The danger in not knowing this information is that you could get discouraged because you think it should sell in a week, when really it will take much longer. Discouraged sellers may eventually list with agents, only to find that the home still doesn't sell.

2. Develop an advertising budget.

It costs money to advertise. Do your research so that you know the cost of advertising and budget and plan accordingly. Find out what the local newspaper or for-sale-by-owner publication charges, and ask about any frequency discounts. Balance these up-front, out-of-pocket costs with the potential commission savings. And remember that many of your expenses may be tax-deductible as selling costs

3. Price your property in line with your market.

An accurate price is critical to your success. If your pricing strategy is to set an initial high price to see if anyone "bites," the only one who will be bitten is you! You will most likely generate the most interest in your home when it first goes on the market - so don't blow your chances with reckless experimentation. Buyers are much more likely to make a reasonable offer on a fairly priced home, and are likely to make no offers on an overpriced home.

The best way to ensure that your home is fairly priced is to get a professional appraisal. For a couple hundred dollars, you will gain the confidence of knowing you've priced your home accurately. Other options include doing your own comparative market analysis, which involves going to the town clerk's office and finding out the selling prices of homes similar to yours.

How much "cushion" or "negotiating room" to build into your price will depend on your specific needs, market conditions and type of property. Buyers prefer buying directly from the owner because they stand to get a better price. Retain your competitive edge over listed houses by pricing your home accurately and competitively.

4. Do your home work.

Buyers will want to buy a good-looking home that suits their needs, at the best price. Buyers want a home that is in "move-in" condition, so do that deferred maintenence.

There is a very simple rule to enhancing your home's appearance: increase the clean, and reduce the clutter. Your home must be clean to sell it. Use commonsense: pack up your collections, your memorabilia, your junk, and make the home sparkle from top to bottom, inside and out, including the windows. The outside of your home its exterior and the yard should be given special attention because buyers will want to do a "drive-by." Buyers will call you up, ask questions about the house and then want to take a look: the drive-by. If your property looks like a dump on the outside, they will just keep on driving! Don't make the mistake of thinking that the buyers will forget about the crummy yard, dead grass, and peeling paint after they fall in love with the interior of your home. You'll never get them out of the car, let alone inside your home, if you don't make the exterior inviting.

5. Effectively advertise & market your home.

In addition to newspaper classified ads, other advertising avenues are for-sale-by-owner publications and a sign in the yard.

According to a recent *USA Today* survey of home buyers, 49% said they found the house they eventually purchased just by seeing a sign in the yard. It's a good idea to invest in a large, sturdy, professionally-made sign that is easy to read and displays your phone number prominently. An attractive, well-constructed sign creates a good first impression. A professional sign tells the buyer that you are serious about selling.

In all your advertising, the more information, the better. Emphasize the selling points: mention that it's offered by owner - a selling point with buyers. Tell the style of home, the number of bedrooms and baths, the general location, the price, any enticements like "below appraisal" or"remodeled", and your telephone number.

If your area has a for-sale-by-owner publication, it is your most cost-effective and best advertising vehicle. These publications allow for relatively lengthy descriptions of the home and for photographs. This advertising vehicle target markets your home specifically to buyers, provides lots of information and the ads have a relatively long life-span (weeks to months) vs. 1 day in a newspaper. The more information a buyer has about your home before they call, the more serious that buyer is likely to be.

Price your home competitively, advertise it effectively, and get ready for the phone to ring!

6. Showing your home.

Showing your home is where you personally interact with the buying public. Probably your first contact with a buyer will be over the telephone, or in response to an ad or your sign in the yard...so plan ahead for probable questions and have good answers. Buyers will have more confidence in you and your home, if your can answer their questions effectively.

It is helpful to prepare a fact sheet about your home that presents the dimensions of the rooms, lot size, heat source, amenities, etc. It is useful to have estimates of utility costs and taxes, and ask a lender to prepare an estimate of the monthly mortgage payment for your home at the prevailing interest rate and standard downpayment amounts. This information should be placed by the telephone along with a pad of paper to keep track of calls, with phone numbers and addresses. Have an answering machine ready to field calls if you're not home. Put a message on it that says the house is for sale and you'd love to show it to them.

When scheduling a visit be sure to give good directions; faulty directions could set a sour mood for the showing. Schedule the visit when you know you'll have enough time to show it in a relaxed and unhurried manner. Remember, you're in control.

Prepare your home by cleaning up and reducing clutter, put on some nice background music, turn on all the lights, open the drapes and curtains, check for unpleasant smells (baking bread is an effective way to create a nice "homey" aroma), and make sure the home is at a comfortable temperature.

When showing the home present the most positive features first, if at all possible. The objective in showing your home is to give the buyers adequate opportunity to imagine themselves living there. Also be sensitive to the fact that some buyers may want to view the home alone - so they can openly discuss their likes and dislikes with each other. If you're giving a guided tour don't talk too much about the home's "warts," don't assume that what you consider a drawback is universal; you could talk yourself out of a sale.

At the end of the visit, answer any of the questions that remain, and give them a copy of the fact sheet as a take-home message about your home. Also, if other buyers are interested in your home mention this fact. Knowing that others are interested could prompt an offer from buyers sitting on the fence. Be sure to follow up with a phone call to buyers a week or so after they've inspected your property. Many sales are made when you call to answer any other questions and offer the opportunity for a subsequent visit.

Above all relax. Many homesellers just like you describe showing their home as being similar to having company over. Both you and the prospective buyer will find the experience helpful and hopefully, enjoyable.

7. Negotiation: Hammering out the deal.

Many sellers are wary of the negotiation process because they make it more that it really is--a dialog between a buyer and seller. We all negotiate everyday--with our spouses, friends, co-workers, children, it's a basic form of human communication.

The number one rule in negotiation is to avoid confrontation. It's not a battle to win. Successful negotiations occur when both the seller and the buyer feel they got what they wanted: a win/win situation. You're both avoiding real estate commissions so you're way ahead already!

Second, plan ahead and know what's subject to negotiation and what isn't. Do you want the washer and dryer, or can you afford to leave it behind and use it as a negotiating tool? Consider these issues ahead of time so you know where you stand.

Third, be willing to compromise. Depending on your situation you may have factored some "negotiating room" in your price. Conceeding a little on price will make the buyer feel good, and may cement the deal.

Fourth, avoid saying no: it ends negotiation. Consider all reasonable requests and thoroughly examine whether the request can be filled to your mutual satisfaction.

At this point the buyer may present to you a Sales Contract, which describes the details of their offer to purchase. You can accept, reject the offer outright, or submit a counteroffer with changes in the terms that fit your needs. Expect to go through several rounds of offer /counteroffer. Before you sign any contract be sure that you have your attorney examine it to make sure that you understand the ramifications of what you are signing and can meet the conditions of the contract.

Many contracts to purchase will have contingencies or conditions attached. For example, most contracts to purchase will be contingent on the buyer qualifying for and getting suitable financing; or on the property appraising for the purchase price or less, or the home passing certain inspections. Failure to meet conditions or terms in the contract may be sufficient reason to invalidate the contract and derail the sale.

Don't be intimidated by negotiation. Many private sale sellers report that negotiation goes very smoothly and really is a non-issue. In fact, some sellers report the development of new friendships with their buyers!

8. Mortgage choices.

It's important for you to know about the buyer's financing options. Since your contract will be probably depend on the buyer getting a mortgage, it might be helpful in some circumstances for you to suggest good financing routes for the buyer. For example, if you know that your home is eligible for special financing, disclosing that information could make the difference in a sale to a buyer with borderline financial strength. Also, some buyers will have very little cash for a down payment despite having sufficient income.

For cash poor buyers it may be an option to obtain loans backed by government agencies such as Federal Housing Authority (FHA) or Veterans Administration. These loans typically require little or no down payment, and sometimes the closing costs can also be financed in the loan. These programs do have some restrictions on property and buyer eligibility, ask your lender for the details. Also, if your mortgage is assumable, this can be a powerful selling point. Check out the details with your lender.

Involve mortgage professionals in the private sale of your home. They can be of great assistance in helping determine the financial strength of the buyers. Furthermore, loan officers have lots of experience in real estate transactions, and can give you tips and suggestions that can make your job easier. And they're motivated to see you succeed, after all, no one needs a new loan until you actually sell your property!

9. Closing the deal.

At the closing the buyer gets title or ownership of the property and you get your equity. Between signing the contract and the closing is when some details need attention. You need to keep track of things so that nothing falls through the cracks and sours the deal. Double-check everything. Find out what lender your buyer is using and make sure that they applied for financing and when they will likely get it. If any inspections were needed, they need to be scheduled and performed. Any resulting repairs will also need to be done. Your buyer's lawyer will conduct a title search to make sure there are no outstanding liens or problems against the property so that the buyer can receive the property free and clear of any of your debt. Any title problems found will be need to be rectified now. Your attorney will prepare the warranty deed for you to transfer the property to the new owner at the closing. Your attorney or lender will help you prepare the necessary documents to bring to the closing.

When thinking about your selling options keep in mind that an attractive, fairly-priced home will virtually *sell itself!* Make the commitment to sell on your own, advertise effectively and show it smartly and you will be on the right path to making the sale...and saving yourself thousands of dollars in commission fees.

The tasks involved in selling a home can be accomplished by a motivated seller with the assistance of key professionals who have a vested interest in guiding the transaction to completion. You are already motivated by the commission savings; attorneys, appraisers, home inspectors and lenders essentially take over, once you find a buyer...so you aren't all alone when selling on your own.

Chapter 12

Steps involved in buying a home

The steps involved in purchasing a home are quite straightforward and can be summarized into three separate concepts: define and refine the type of property you are looking for, find the money to purchase it and fulfill the terms and conditions of the written Purchase and Sales Contract.

Narrow down what you are looking for: Take a few moments to discuss what you're looking for with your spouse or partner before you start setting up appointments to look at properties. Make a list of "Must have" features together, then discuss other "Would like, but can live without" features. After you've looked at a dozen or so properties, re-evaluate your criteria. Often priorities shift with time and what was an earlier definite "must-have" feature is now re-classified as "desirable, but can live without feature."

How much can you afford? Have a realistic idea of how much you can afford before you start looking (most lenders will pre-qualify you for free, ask the seller he probably can refer you to a good lender). Not only will this save time, but will also avoid needless disappointment on everyone's part.

Don't use agents, they're unnecessary. Don't bring an agent with you to look at for-sale-by-owner properties, or bring them into the picture when it's time to draw up a contract, unless you are willing to pay their commission through either a higher sales price, or out of your own pocket. Otherwise, you may risk losing the house. (note: your lawyer can help you if you aren't sure of the process).

If you're also looking at listed properties with an agent don't sign a contract that locks you into looking with only him or her, or guarantees them a commission even if you find the house yourself! Specify that a commission be paid only if you buy a property shown to you by that agent. This enables you to look with others, and also at for-sale-by-owner properties, at your own convenience.

Sell my current house first or buy, then sell? If you find the house you want to buy before you've sold your present home, and the seller is reluctant to sign a contract with you with the contingency that you sell your home first, you may draw up a contract that allows the seller to continue marketing and advertising the property yet gives you the "first right of refusal" should he receive another offer. This way you will be notified immediately if the seller has another offer, giving you an opportunity to re-offer if necessary. Another option is to put a non-refundable deposit on the property. This shows the sellers that you are serious about buying their property and this could sway them into accepting your offer over other competing offers.

If you sell your house before finding a home you want to buy, be sure your sales contract is contingent upon you, the seller, finding suitable housing! There are stories of homesellers frantic to find a home under pressure, and even having to rent after the closing, because they sold first. Remember, the sellers are legally bound to sell once the contract is signed.

Present your offer to the sellers. Present the offer in writing. Many sellers will have the necessary legal forms and contracts. You simply fill in the blanks with the information that is pertinent to your sale. Of course, before you sign the offer to purchase you would want to have it reviewed by a real estate attorney. When presenting an offer, be courteous and respectful of the sellers. In general, avoid criticizing the property with statements like "we don't care for the new carpeting, and therefore will have to replace it." This will not justify a lower offer and may possibly insult the sellers, decreasing your chances of their accepting your offer.

Include a deposit check with the written offer. Most deposits are in the range of 1 to 3% of the sales price. This, of course, is up to you. In general, the larger the deposit you include with your written offer, the more likely the seller is to accept your offer.

If you are unsure about the value of the property you are going to make an offer on you can make your offer contingent upon the property appraising for the selling price or higher. This is a common contingency that is required by the lender that is underwriting the mortgage on the property. They want to make sure that the value of the property will cover the amount of their mortgage interest in the property.

Walk-through inspection. Request that you be permitted to walk-through the house (shortly before closing) after the furniture is removed to make sure that some of the home's faults weren't covered with furniture, rugs, or wall coverings. It is far easier to correct any problems or arrange for necessary repair work before the house is sold than afterwards.

Know the condition of the property. Request that the seller complete a property disclosure form, stating the condition of the major aspects of the property, before you make an offer. Here the seller would complete a Property Disclosure Form, or similar document.

If you don't know much about building construction, don't worry. Simply make your offer contingent upon the property passing a professional housing inspection. This is also an excellent way to become more familiar with the current condition and maintenance needs of your future home.

How long can the sellers consider your offer? Give the sellers a reasonable amount of time to consider your offer. (24 hrs is common.) Also, don't make the deadline time at midnight unless you usually are awake at that time!

Real estate contracts must be in writing. Misunderstandings can occur if you rely on memory when coming to terms about your real estate purchase. If the seller says they will clean up the mess behind the shed before you move in, get it in writing. Put everything in writing. Your sales contract should spell out whether the washer and dryer stay, when you will notify the seller about the status of your financing, etc.

You've made an offer on a home, now what?

First of all, relax. Once you find a home that you want you just need to stay on top of a few details and the process will proceed along course. Your attorney or the attorney (or closing officer) of your mortgage company will be gathering most of the required paperwork and forms for the closing as an integral part of the loan process. To finalize the sale , you and the seller will probably work with a third party, usually an attorney or escrow officer , to handle deposits, documents and instructions necessary to complete your home purchase. This period of time between when the offer is accepted and the deal closes is known as the escrow period. Escrow can be a trying time, but if the sales contract isn't loaded with unusual contingencies, and buyer and seller work together, expect the process to take one to two months.

During escrow, you'll help the attorney or closing officer remove contingencies, prorate property tax payments, record and exchange deeds, work to clear the title and record and exchange the deed, among other tasks.

Opening escrow

Generally, here's what you can expect during the escrow period. An escrow account is opened with a title company, or with an attorney or the lender's escrow department. Which one is used really depends on local custom and procedure. In general, in the eastern United States attorneys or mortgage companies tend to perform this function, while in the west, title companies or escrow officers perform this task. As with finding any qualified professional, ask people you trust for referrals to an attorney, closing officer or escrow officer.

First, the buyer's check (the deposit) will be deposited into the escrow account, this check should accompanies the written offer. Area custom dictates who - the buyer or the seller - opens the account. Also file any additional documents related to the transaction (such as the Purchase & Sale Agreement). Deposits into this account will be applied to the purchase price, or returned if the deal should fall through. At this point, it's the buyer's responsibility (or the buyer's attorney) to order title insurance (which protects the buyer and the lender against unknown claims on the title) and most likely a preliminary title search report to determine if there are any claims currently against the title. The lender will require the buyer do so.

Title reports

When you and the seller have signed the Purchase and Sale contract, a buyer can order a preliminary title report. The report summarizes the condition of the title, including any liens against the property, encumbrances or claims (say a second mortgage) against the title and easements. Should a problem be found learning about it early in the process will give ample time to correct it so that the closing is not held up.

You must resolve any claims against the title, such as liens or judgments, which could threaten your right to title, and ownership of the property.

Other problems that crop up very rarely are newly discovered easements, lawsuits disputing the boundary line, law suits filed against the sellers, common interest development covenants, conditions and restrictions and /or an unknown heir could appear and lay claim to the property. If any of these conditions exist, it will require legal assistance to resolve. If the title report uncovers items that cannot immediately be resolved the buyer can back out of the sale, negotiate with for a remedy, or buy the home with an imperfect title.

Clear, marketable or unencumbered title

If the title search report reveals a clear title, the title company or lender may check once again to produce a final report to be sure no claims were made against the title during the escrow period.

Contingencies

The Purchase and Sale contract likely contains contingencies (items/ tasks that must be completed before the deal can progress), and each one is said to be removed or released when the item has been answered or resolved. Common contingencies include general home inspections, roof inspections, termite inspections, completing a related home sale and evidence of adequate financing.

If, for example, the buyer can't obtain adequate financing in the time prescribed, the seller can back out or negotiate with the buyer to extend the escrow period. This is also known as a Purchase and Sale contract extension. The seller may want assurance that you are working in good faith and can ask for an increase in deposit or some other concession on your part. Likewise if the offer was contingent upon the seller repairing termite damage, but the buyer didn't schedule and perform the work in a timely fashion, the seller could back out of the deal or negotiate with you to correct the problem. So if you put contingencies into a Purchase and Sale contract make sure that if that contingency requires you to do something by a certain date that you do it, or risk losing the house to another buyer.

Closing escrow, or closing the sale

A few days before escrow is scheduled to close, the buyer has a right to inspect the property, looking for any changes that may have occurred since the Purchase and Sales contract was signed. They buyer will want to make sure fixtures, appliances, window coverings and other agreed upon items are still in place and that all are in good working order.

If the buyer discovers problems, he or she can insist on delaying the closing until the problem is remedied, go ahead and close with a credit from the seller to remedy the problem,or decide the problem doesn't warrant further delay. Some of the remaining paperwork that you will be asked to sign before the closing includes, final escrow instructions, settlement sheet of disbursements or settlement statement, copy of the preliminary title report, deed of trust and other lender forms, copies of inspection reports, tax statements, and a rental agreement if you will live in the home for some time after close. The deal will close when thc new deed is recorded in the buyer's name, the seller is paid for the home, and other monies that are due the seller and others are paid. On rare occassions money may be requested to be held in escrow after the closing, to pay any contractors or other vendors for unfinished work.

These steps will vary based on regional customs. Please ask your attorney or mortgage lender for further information.

Buyer's remorse

Many homebuyers will have second-thoughts about buying the house shortly after making the offer or at some time during the period of time leading up to the closing. This is commonly know as buyer's remorse. Buyer's remorse is completely normal and most homeowners experience it to some degree. Buying a home is such a major life changing event that there are bound to be many emotions associated with it. Thinking that you may have made a big mistake, that you're getting in over your head or that the new home will just be too much responsibility are common thoughts for even the most experienced homeowners. Don't let this throw you. You've done your research and have found a new home that will give you many years of enjoyment and form the basis of lots of happy memories. Enjoy it!

Index